THE LAST MAN

TWENTIETH-CENTURY CONTINENTAL FICTION

THE
LAST MAN

by MAURICE BLANCHOT

translated by Lydia Davis

New York   COLUMBIA UNIVERSITY PRESS   1987

Columbia University Press wishes to express its appreciation of assistance given by the government of France through le Ministère de la Culture in the preparation of this translation.

Library of Congress Cataloging-in-Publication Data

Blanchot, Maurice.
The last man.

Translation of: Le dernier homme.
I. Title.
PQ2603.L3343D413   1987   843'.912   87-5192
ISBN 0-231-06244-3

Book design by Laiying Chong.

Columbia University Press
New York   Guildford, Surrey

© 1987 Columbia University Press
French original: *Le dernier homme* © 1957 Editions Gallimard
All rights reserved

I

A S SOON AS I was able to use that word, I said what I
must always have thought of him: that he was the last
man. In truth, almost nothing distinguished him from the
others. He was more retiring, but not modest, imperious
when he wasn't talking; then, in silence, one had to attribute
to him thoughts which he gently rejected; this could be read in
his eyes, which questioned us with surprise, with distress:
why is that all you think? Why can't you help me? His eyes
were pale, of a silvery pallor, like a child's eyes. In fact, there
was something childish about his face, an expression that
invited us to be considerate, but also to feel vaguely protec-
tive.

Certainly he talked very little, but his silence often went
unnoticed. I believed that he had a kind of discretion, sometimes that he was a little scornful, sometimes that he with-
drew too much into himself or outside of us. Now I think that
maybe he didn't always exist or that he didn't yet exist. But

I'm also thinking of something more extraordinary: he had a simplicity that didn't surprise us.

Yet he was disturbing. He disturbed me more than others. Maybe he changed everyone's condition, maybe only mine. Maybe he was the most useless, the most superfluous of all people.

And what if he hadn't said to me, one day, "I can't think about myself: there is something terrible there, a difficulty that slips away, an obstacle that can't be met"?

And right afterward: "He says he can't think about himself: about others, still, about one other, but it's like an arrow coming from too far away that won't reach the target, and yet when it stops and falls, the target quivers in the distance and comes to meet it."

At these times, he talks very fast in a sort of low voice: great sentences that seem infinite, that roll with the sound of waves, an all-encompassing murmur, a barely perceptible planetary song. This goes on and on, is terribly imposing in its gentleness and distance. How to answer? Listening to it, who wouldn't have the feeling of being that target?

He wasn't addressing anyone. I don't mean he wasn't speaking to me, but someone other than me was listening to him, someone who was perhaps richer, vaster, and yet more singular, almost too general, as though, confronting him, what had been "I" had strangely awakened into a "we," the presence and united force of the common spirit. I was a little more, a little less than myself: more, in any case, than all men. In this "we," there is the earth, the power of the elements, a sky that is not this sky, there is a feeling of loftiness and calm, there is also the bitterness of an obscure constraint. All of this is I before him, and he seems almost nothing at all.

There were reasons for me to fear him, to dream endlessly of his ruin, I wanted to persuade him to disappear, I would have liked to make him admit that he didn't doubt himself, an admission that would probably have annihilated me, I surrounded him with attention, calculations, hope, suspicion, forgetfulness, and finally pity, but I always protected him from the curiosity of the others. I didn't draw attention to him. He was strangely weak and vulnerable where that was concerned. A superficial glance directed at his person seemed to expose him to an incomprehensible menace. A profound look, capable of seeking him out where he was, did not trouble him, troubled him less. Down there, he was too light, too carefree, too dispersed. Down there, I don't know what could have reached him, or whom one would still have reached, in him.

There are moments when I recover him as he must have been: a certain word I read, write, moves aside to make room for his own word. I can tell that he has fallen silent at a certain moment, that at another he has taken notice of me. I pass in front of his room; I hear him coughing—like a wolf, he said—and in fact it was a cold sort of groaning, an odd noise, severe, rather savage. I was never mistaken about his step: somewhat slow, quiet and even, more labored than one would have thought from his great lightness, but not heavy, only causing one to imagine, even when he was advancing down the long hallway, that he was always climbing a flight of stairs, that he was coming from very far down, very far away, and that he was still very far away. True, I hear him not only when he stops at my door, but also when he doesn't stop. It's hard to judge: is he still coming? Is he already going away? The ear doesn't know; only the heartbeat discloses it.

His near stammering. With disconcerting promptness one word hid behind another. He hesitates almost imperceptibly; he hesitates almost constantly; only his hesitation allows me to be somewhat sure of myself, and to listen to him, answer him. Yet there was something else: something like a canal lock would open and we would change levels in relation to each other.

Docile, almost obedient, almost submissive, and contradicting very seldom, not arguing, almost never blaming us and prepared to consent naively to everything that had to be done. I believe there were days when the simplest person would have found him too simple and when chatting about the most unimportant things occupied him completely, gave him a pleasure people don't understand: though not with everyone, or only with everyone? The happiness of saying yes, of endlessly affirming.

I became convinced that I had first known him when he was dead, then when he was dying. Passing in front of his door, they gave me this image of him:

"This is a room you'll be able to have."

When, afterward, at certain moments, I was in some sense forced to speak of him in the past, I again saw the door of that room, occupied, they said, by someone who had just died, and it seemed to me he returned to that moment when he was only a dead man making room for a living. Why that past? Did it bring me closer to him? Did it make him more discernible by giving me the strength to look him in the face, present, though in a mirror? Or am I the one in the past? This feeling—"I see him," and immediately, "I saw him, therefore he doesn't see me"—injected into our relations the torment of an unspoken distress. I would have liked never to leave him alone, solitude made me afraid for him, as did the nights, the idea that he was sleeping, that he wasn't sleeping. I think he never dreamed. That is horrifying too—a sleep that is never altogether closed, that is open on one side: a sleep I imagined by thinking of the blackness under one's eyelids that fades, whitens a little when one dies, so that to die might be to see, for a moment.

If I ask myself: did he think more than you think? I see only his spirit of lightness, which made him innocent of the worst. A creature so irresponsible, so terribly not guilty, like a madman, but without a speck of madness, or else hiding that madness inside him, always infallible: he was a burn in the eyes. One had to draw him into a fault, one had to reinvent for him alone the lost sense of what a fault was. He would express some thoughts: how light they are, how they immediately rise, nothing disturbs them, nothing imposes them.

"But isn't that what makes them bitter?"

"Bitter? Slightly bitter."

He gave me the feeling of eternity, of a person who would need no justification. I went back to positing a God, the better to see them as invisible to each other. He enriched me with my own ignorance, I mean he added something to me that I don't know. The moment we met, I was lost to myself, but I also lost much more, and the surprising thing is that I struggle, that I can still struggle to get it back. Where does that come from? Where does it come from that in the space where I am, where he has brought me, I constantly go back near the point where everything could start up again as though with a new beginning? For this, it would be enough to . . . He says it would be enough if, in fact, I stopped struggling.

If he was so strong, it wasn't that he was invulnerable. On the contrary, his was a weakness that went beyond us. Yes, it surpassed what we could bear: it was actually terrible, he inspired terror, much more so than someone absolutely powerful would have done, but it was a rather gentle terror and, for a woman, tender and violent. To offend him was perhaps not possible for me, but the idea of offending him filled me with anguish: it was like throwing a stone that would never be thrown back to me, a shaft that did not strike me. I didn't know whom I was wounding, nor what this wound was, it could not be shared by anyone, nor heal over in anyone else, it would be a sore to the very end. And more than anything else his immeasurable weakness: this was what I didn't have the courage to approach, even if only by knocking up against it.

Often, what he told of his story was so obviously borrowed from books that, warned immediately by a kind of suffering, one made great efforts to avoid hearing him. It was here that his desire to talk miscarried most strangely. He did not have any precise notion of what we call the seriousness of facts. The truthfulness, the exactness of what has to be said astonished him. Each time, this surprise was indicated and dissembled by a rapid flutter of his eyelids.

"Now what do they mean by *event*?"—I read the question in his recoil. I don't think his weakness could tolerate the hardness there is in our lives when they are recounted, he couldn't even imagine it. Or hadn't anything real ever happened to him—an emptiness he concealed and illuminated by random stories? Nevertheless, here and there a correct note sounded, like a cry from behind the mask, revealing someone who eternally asked for help without being able to indicate where he was.

For some, he was curiously easy to approach; for others, he was surrounded by an innocence that was marvelously smooth on the outside, but on the inside composed of a thousand tiny edges of very hard crystal, so that at the slightest attempt to approach him he risked being torn by the long, fine needles of his innocence. He was there, slightly withdrawn, talking very little, with very poor and very ordinary words; he was almost buried in the armchair, disturbingly motionless, his large hands hanging, tired, from the ends of his arms. Yet one hardly looked at him; one saved looking at him for later. When I picture him this way: was he a broken man? On his way downhill from the very beginning? What was he waiting for? What did he hope to save? What could we do for him? Why did he suck in each of our words so avidly? Are you altogether forsaken? Can't you speak for yourself? Must we think in your absence, die in your place?

He needed something firm to sustain him. But I suffered over everything that seemed to shut him in. I became anxious, agitated. It was this agitation that removed me from myself, putting in my place a more general being, sometimes "we," sometimes what was vaguest and most indecisive. Then we suffered over being such a great number before him who was so alone, we suffered over being connected to one another by so many bonds—mediocre, but strong, and necessary, and foreign to him. Later, I missed those first moments. I did not cease to be hampered, in my attempt to see him, by him and by what I still wanted to recognize of myself in him.

He didn't make my life easy; he was so important and he was so insignificant. One could persuade oneself he was hiding something, that he was hiding himself. It is always more comforting to assume there is a secret behind what torments you, but that secret thing was actually hiding in us. No doubt we surprised him, but he lacked the concern for himself that would have allowed him to be curious about us. And curiosity was the fault we couldn't commit against him; he appealed with such gentleness for discretion, the reserve of closed eyes; he asked for that, that one not see him, that one not see how much we had already disappeared from his eyes, how hard it was for him not to look upon us as inhabitants of the other shore. Later I clearly saw he had only turned to me in order to be in more gentle communication with that thought; it had become too strong, it had to be tested. I think the need to end spoke to him more and more imperiously.

Can one live close to someone who listens passionately to everything? It wears you out, burns you. One wants a little indifference; one appeals for forgetfulness; true, forget-fulness was always there; before the passionate depth of forgetfulness, then, one had to talk without pausing, with-out stopping.

He wasn't a stranger to us; on the contrary, he was close to us with a closeness that seemed like a mistake. He fought confidently, in a way I can't imagine, to maintain the ease of daily relations with us. And yet how difficult it was for me actually to think of him: by myself, I couldn't manage it, I had to appeal, in myself, to others. He seemed above all else afraid of not treating us with enough consideration, speak-ing to us, falling silent as though tentatively, by intuition. He must have known that for us he represented an ordeal, and he did his best to make it as light as possible for us. He was there, that was enough, he was there as one of us, that was certainly the limit of tact, unless that wariness was the very thing we felt exposed to. The strangest thing was that we had the feeling, all of us, that we just barely sufficed for his presence and that one alone would not have kept him there, not that he was too imposing, but, on the contrary, because he needed to be disregarded. He needed to be one too many: one more, only one more.

Yet we also resisted him, we resisted him almost con-stantly. As I dwelled on it, I came to believe that there was a circle around us which he couldn't cross. There were parts of us where he didn't touch us, certainties he didn't have ac-cess to, thoughts we didn't allow him to think. He wasn't to see us as we were, nor were we to be tempted to find out what he didn't see of us. But it isn't easy to conceal yourself from the sort of attention that becomes so distracted it drops you as soon as it has grasped you. And maybe each of us, by preserving what was most central to us, was only trying to show it to him—out of some need to put it under his protection, as though in safe custody. What would I have wanted to withdraw from him, what certain thing would I have had to make altogether uncertain for him? I answered myself immediately: him, only him. But at the same time it seems to me I gave myself a completely different answer.

Perhaps he was among us: at first, among all of us. He didn't separate us, he maintained a certain emptiness that we didn't want to fill up, it was something to respect, maybe to love. When someone stops speaking it is hard not to go looking for the missing thought, but even though his thought often called out to us, one couldn't do such violence to him, he fell silent with such great innocence, such obvious lack of responsibility, he fell silent absolutely and entirely. That didn't call for help, it didn't cause any embarrassment, it gently killed time. He was among us and yet he had hidden preferences, unpredictable impulses that suddenly thrust him back a great distance, not only indifferent to those who were there, but causing us to be indifferent to ourselves and withdrawing us from the people closest to us. A storm that changed us into a desert, a silent storm. But who are we after that, how do we find ourselves with ourselves again, how do we love one who wasn't loved during that terrible moment?

I think a reverie comes from him to us, one that agitates us, deceives us, opens us to the suspicion of a thought that won't seem to let itself be thought. I often asked myself if he wasn't communicating to us, without his knowledge and against our wishes, something of that thought. I listened to those very simple words, I listen to his silence, I learn about his weakness, I follow him softly everywhere he would like me to, but he has already killed curiosity, erased it, I don't know who I am, I who question him, he leaves me more ignorant, dangerously overwhelmed with ignorance. Maybe we didn't have the correct feelings for him, the feelings that would have allowed the approach of what he revealed to us. What feelings? What could be born of me, for him? There is something terrible about imagining that I should have felt something I'm unaware of, that I was bound by impulses I have no notion of. At least this much is true: I never tried to discover these new feelings in myself. And once he was there, his simplicity did not consent to anything strange, anything I could not have said of someone else as well. It was a sort of secret rule that I was obliged to observe.

The thought which is spared me at each moment: that he, the last man, is nevertheless not the last.

I only noticed by degrees that he turned me away from myself. He didn't demand any attention from me, he demanded less than a thought. It was this *less* that was strongest. I owed him a limitless distraction, and even less, the opposite of expectation, the reverse of faith, which wasn't doubt: ignorance and neglect. But this still wasn't enough: this ignorance had to ignore even me and leave me to one side, gently, uncertainly, without any sense of exclusion or aversion. Then who was encountering him? Who was talking to him? Who wasn't thinking of him? I didn't know, I only felt that it was never I.

Even a God needs a witness. The divine incognito needs to be perceived down here. I had spent a long time imagining what his witness would be. I would become almost ill at the thought that I would have to be that witness, a creature who not only had to exclude himself from himself in favor of that end, but exclude himself from that end without favor and remain as closed, as motionless as a milestone on a road. I myself spent a lot of time, a hard time, a time of suffering, becoming something close to a milestone. But slowly—abruptly—the thought occurred to me that this story had no witness: I was there—the "I" was already no more than a Who?, a whole crowd of Who?s—so that there would be no one between him and his destiny, so that his face would remain bare and his gaze undivided. I was there, not in order to see him, but so that he wouldn't see himself, so that it would be me he saw in the mirror, someone other than him—another, a stranger, nearby, gone, the shadow of the other shore, no one—and that in this way he would remain a man until the very end. He wasn't to split in two. This is the great temptation of those who are approaching their end: they look at themselves and talk to themselves; they turn themselves into a solitude peopled by themselves—the emptiest, the most false. But if I was present, he would be the most alone of all men, without even himself, without that last man which he was—and thus he would be the very last. This was certainly capable of frightening me—such great duties, such naked feelings, such excessive cares. I could not respond except with carelessness, the motion of the days, the refusal to reveal him—to myself or to him.

If, in my memory, he is now a man I look at as though I saw only him, that importance is no measure of him. It only indicates the constraint I exercise in order to grasp him, the falsification of our relations, my weakness in not being able to conceive of him or recall him except as important. I know that in doing this I am betraying everything. How would he have been able to turn away the slightest particle of my life? Maybe he is there, in a room whose lighted window I see. He is a man alone, a stranger, gravely ill. For a long time now he has not left his bed, he doesn't move, he doesn't speak. I question no one about this, I'm not sure what is said refers to the man I picture to myself. He seems to me completely forgotten. This forgetting is the element I breathe when I go down the hall. I understand why, when he resumed taking his meals with us, we were surprised by his gentle, retiring face, a face which wasn't gloomy, but quite the contrary, radiant, of a radiant near-invisibility. We were seeing the face of forgetting. It can certainly be forgotten, in fact it asks to be forgotten, and yet it concerns us all.

I have spoken of his hidden preferences. This created an element of mystery. Each of us, I think, felt that someone else was the intended object of his preferences, not just any-one else, but always the closest one, as though he was only able to look by looking slightly elsewhere, choosing the per-son one was touching, one was brushing against, the person who, in truth, one had been convinced one was, until then. Maybe he always chose someone else in us. Maybe, by this choice, he made each of us into someone else. It was the look by which he would most have wanted to be observed, but which perhaps never observed us, still gazed only at a little emptiness near us. One day, this emptiness was a young woman I was close to. I had no doubt about this gaze, which had come to rest on her with all the force of something distant, had fixed on her, chosen her. But everything leads me to believe that as far as she was concerned, I was the one who had been chosen. I often had the impression that, close as we were, we were also drawn together by misunder-standing.

She had been here several years when I came. In her eyes, therefore, I had been a newcomer, an ignorant creature crossing the threshold in all the confusion of having being uprooted. This made her smile, but it was attractive too. When he came, I, in turn, was an old fellow. She called him "the professor." Maybe he was much older than we, who were among the youngest; he once told her he was thirty-eight. A little later I stayed for a time in a place high in the mountains. When I came back, he was, they told me, almost dead; they hadn't seen him for a long time. I found she had not changed much. She seemed to me even younger than I remembered, also closer, though more separate. She had in some way locked herself up in this place, she had a relationship of understanding with it that allowed her to extract from it a lively, secret truth, whereas the others were still looking back at the regret, the hope, and the despair of another life. I wasn't really from here or from back there, but on my return I was struck by how amazing it was to meet her again and yet as though by chance, a happiness that seemed to have continued in my absence and without my knowing it, all the while preserving the lightness of a whim. A whim? But a free one, a chance meeting that owed nothing except to chance. It is often said of two people united by very little: there is nothing between them. Well, the fact was there was nothing between us, and no one between us, not even ourselves.

Then winter came. The snow gave certain people something resembling a second illness, but for a few others it was a sort of relief and distraction from their pain. I'm not saying he was recuperating. He seemed to me much weaker than when he had arrived. He walked with a slight hesitation; his very strange step created the impression that only for moments at a time did he stop at our level, but that he came from very far down and that it was always by virtue of a gentle stubbornness that he came. And yet these weren't the motions of a man about to fall: it was a different uncertainty, which caused one to become unsure of oneself, an uncertainty that was sometimes painful, sometimes light and a little drunk. I also noticed how much his voice must have changed. I thought it was only weaker, but what it said disturbed me because of a difficulty I could not overcome. He was certainly very polite, he paid wonderful attention to everything and everyone; when he drew near, you entered a space where whatever you valued most was accepted, protected, and silently judged in a way that did not say you were right, but made you hope for a kind of justice. Yet he was not easy, nor indulgent, nor good. Actually, I believe he was the hardest thing a man could come up against. Was that because of his distant air, the fact that one had to identify him with some misfortune or other? Despite oneself, one saw him as an enemy. That was the most bitter part of it. How could one have such weakness as one's adversary? How could one fight such naked powerlessness? The anguish this caused was boundless.

Apologizing sadly, he told someone: "Yes, I know I exert a great attraction." At times he seemed very close, at times not close: the walls were down; at times, still very close, but without any connection, the walls were down, not only the walls that separate, but also those that serve to transmit signals, the language of prisons. Then a wall had to be raised again, a little indifference had to be asked of him, that calm distance in which people's lives find their equilibrium. I think she always had the strength to leave him at a certain distance from himself. She had a simplicity that protected both of them. She accepted with naturalness even what became terrible, she wasn't startled by it; and if she had to allude to it, it was in order to bring it into the familiarity of words. I was surprised by the way she would start talking about herself when he was there and as soon as he was there again: very lightly, without saying anything important; she did not come forward. But how the word *I* vibrated between her teeth, passing like a breath, a calm violence, through her closed mouth! It was as though some instinct had told her that in his presence she should say *I*, only *I*, that he was fascinated by this light word over which she herself had so few rights and which she spoke in such a way that it almost designated someone else. Maybe all *I*'s were beckoning to him; maybe, through this word alone, everyone had the power to tell him something important; but she made it closer to him, more intimate. She was *me* for him, and yet in some sense it was a *me* adrift, an open *me* which didn't remember anyone.

That *I*—this is what I can't say—was terrible: terribly gentle and weak, terribly naked and without decency, a tremor alien to all pretense, altogether pure of me, but of a purity that went to the far end of everything, that demanded everything, that revealed and delivered over what was altogether dark, maybe the last *I*, the one that will astonish death, the one that death draws to itself like the secret that is forbidden it, a piece of flotsam, a still-living footprint, a mouth open in the sand.

I won't say he separated us: on the contrary; but in this way he separated us and connected us so as to go dangerously beyond us. He took his meals at a little table a short distance away from us because he ate only foods that were almost liquid, and ate them very slowly, with extreme patience. He tolerated everything. He made invisible what efforts were required of him to achieve this, and maybe he no longer had to make any efforts, maybe he tolerated himself so completely, with such a dependable wearing down and a constancy so exact that there was nothing left for him to tolerate, except an emptiness I didn't want to imagine. This was no doubt why he incited us to believe that there had been no events in his life except for one, something abject, monumental, that had driven him to the point where he was, or something neither grandiose nor excessive, maybe something that would have seemed to us quite insignificant but had brought such pressure to bear on him that all other events were volatilized by it. When he ate even more slowly—and it was almost as though he had allowed air and time to take his place struggling through things—she went to him. She sat down more or less next to him, not quite at his table; she sensed, she said, an obscure agitation as soon as she approached, not in his person—he didn't have enough strength for that, and therefore always seemed calm and in control of himself—but in the space next to him: a correction, a silent transformation; he quickly modified his way of seeing and seeing her, he secretly adjusted it: to accommodate her? But not only her, to accommodate everything or maybe chance.

"By coming here, was he perhaps precipitated into a world that was too different?"

But he didn't really have any world, that was why she tried to give him hers, and she really had to be prepared to put up with the consequences. She must have bothered him: yes, simply because he needed all his attention to eat without swallowing the wrong way, but she didn't stop there, she lightly passed over that difficulty, she didn't even want to help him, and yet she also helped him, she caused him to move quietly into a relatively solid place, she connected him to a fixed point, and she sensed how much he was tugging at the mooring rope, but she held fast, she talked to him rapidly, evenly, almost without respite, her eyes seeming fixed on herself, and it was then that something in her speech changed and at its surface came again and again the breath of that fascinating *I* toward which he gradually turned and remained expectant.

What was he? What power had driven him there? Which side was he on? What could one do for him? It was odd that one was tempted to attribute to him the strongest thoughts, the richest intuitions, areas of knowledge we couldn't imagine, an entire, extraordinary experience, whereas we only touched on the strangeness of his weakness. Surely he was capable of thinking everything, knowing everything, but he was also nothing. He had the weakness of an absolutely unhappy man, and that measureless weakness struggled against the force of that measureless thought, that weakness always seemed to find that great thought insufficient, and it demanded this, that what had been thought in such a strong way should be thought again and rethought on the level of extreme weakness. What did that mean? She questioned me about him, as though I had actually been him, and at the same time she said that I was pushing her toward him, she said, too, that she was drawn to him, that she felt closer to him than to anyone else, she went on to say that he frightened her, but almost immediately that he didn't frighten her at all, that she had a sort of confidence in him, a feeling of friendship for him, which she didn't have for me.

It is certainly true that without her, I might never have had the strength actually to think of him. It is also true that she not only made me think, but allowed me not to think of him myself. What I said, thought, at her request, was, rather, a kind of sleep in her, resting in her own life, in my liking for her, it was only her face, the look she gave me. To say that she served as our intermediary would not be correct. She did not serve me in any way, and I wouldn't have consented to make use of her, even for such an end. But, because of her un-affected spontaneity and her lively familiarity, she must have helped me, in my relations with him, to free me of myself, and I experienced a certain happiness limiting my thoughts to her, though they were directed at him. There was something terrible about it, but it was still happy, it was spoken for that body and for that mouth talking to me so tangibly. Maybe it was a dangerously thoughtless move on my part. Maybe I was very much to blame for not worrying more about what became of my thoughts in her, about the weight they obliged her to bear and, even more, about the emptiness they ac-cumulated there, an emptiness that fed on her strength and fearlessness. That is true. But she, too, gave me her thoughts without reflecting, without reckoning, without worrying about either herself or me, she said she only thought them in me and near me, sometimes without saying anything, in a silence that weighed on me to the point of suffocation, but that I left intact.

Certainly she had a kind of power to approach him that I didn't have. She was the first to find a name for what was happening to him—to her, to him, to us all—but it was in me that she thought she first experienced it, she said:

"It's strange, I'm not as sure of you anymore."

"You were sure of me?"

"Yes, you were so motionless, you would be looking at a single point, I always found you in front of that point." As she said this, she looked, not at me, but in the direction of the table, on which there were some written pages; beyond was the wall, beyond the wall other rooms, all alike, rather large, hers too. So now I wasn't motionless any longer?

"Oh, yes; maybe too motionless for the others, who move. It's a terrible thing to imagine that you can't leave that point, that you devote all your strength to it, and perhaps that point isn't fixed."

I tried to recall that point. I could have told her truthfully that that point was also her. The desire to be with her passed through that point, it was my horizon. But when she added, with a sort of pride that kindled the brilliant, almost avid gaze she sometimes had:

"I'm not sure of myself, either," I protested strongly:

"Well, I'm sure of you, I'm sure of nothing but you"— which she listened to with an air of interest, looking at me as though to find out if I was really talking about her. I confirmed it by adding:

"You don't want to deceive yourself, you see things as they are." She immediately asked me:

"And you?"

"I only see what you see, I trust you."

Violently, she went to another extreme: "You don't see anything at all? Yet you think differently from me, you have your own view of things, I'm always aware of that different way of thinking."

Was this a fault? Was she reproaching me for it?

"No, no," she said. "I trust you too."

Then I said something rather crude to her: "I know you will never lie." But that life preserver couldn't keep us afloat for long.

Yet I didn't expect anything. Now she lived in my room almost constantly: close to me, close to the thought that was in me? Sometimes it seemed to me she was watching me, not with any baneful intention or for the purpose of discovering what I might have hidden from her; she was incapable of such subterfuges. Rather, she was looking after my thought, looking after its integrity, giving it the silence it needed, concealing it from everything else, expecting from that thought the feverish familiarity which she wanted to tumble into. The worst part of the winter was upon us then. Because my room was between hers and the professor's, we would hear his cough at night, among all the other coughs, that wild sound that was sometimes a sort of moan, sometimes a triumphant shout, a howl that did not seem to come from such a weak creature, but from an entire horde that stood close to him and passed through him: "Like a wolf," he said. Yes, it was a terrifying noise that I had to shield her from, but that she was waiting for, that she said she could hear coming out of me, crossing me, passing from me to her, reaching her with a force that shook her, that she did not resist. Then came the silence, a moment of happy calm in which everything was forgotten.

It was at about this time that he ceased to be able to talk. He continued, though irregularly, to come down to the rooms on the ground floor, at least to the drawing room, since there was no longer any question of his taking his meals with the others. He didn't seem much more ill, perhaps more at risk, but in a way that didn't actually concern him. I couldn't say he was becoming strange, but the word she had used for me, that I was less sure, fit him too. Yet there was something else, a feeling of increased distress, along with greater power, a repulsion at our approach that kept us at a distance, stopped us from looking at him, but also from appearing embarrassed by looking at him. That his whole person was a mask—this wasn't a new idea, I had already thought of it. Nor did I stop at the thought that this mask was beginning to slip, allowing one to see what he was. But behind this body and this life, I sensed the great pressure exerted by what I thought of as his extreme weakness as it tried to break the dam protecting us from him. I had sometimes noticed a rapid change in level as he was speaking. What he said changed meaning, was no longer directed at us, but at him, at someone other than him, another space, the intimacy of his weakness, the wall, as I said to the young woman—"he has touched the wall"—and what was most striking then was the threat that his quite ordinary words seemed to represent for him, as though they risked unclothing him before the wall, and he expressed this by an obliteration that whitened what he said even as he prepared to say it. This didn't always happen, but it may have been what led us to believe, when he spoke, that he was listening, that he was still listening to us in a marvelous way, to us and all things and also what was more than us, the restless and infinite agitation of the emptiness around us, which he continued to acknowledge.

He did not fail to talk to her, and she did not fail to talk to him, to go up to him resolutely as soon as she saw him. The two of them would remain at a slight distance, in an alcove near the piano. No one paid much attention to them. That she was so young, full of such lively and happy youth, while he was a man not very old yet strangely ruined—this incongruity did not give rise to comment. One imagined that she was filling an official role which she assumed voluntarily because of the length of time she had been here, and which consisted of maintaining a sense of life around those people who were most neglected. Everyone also knew that we were friends. Because of that bond, her other friendships were hardly visible. And really, even in my eyes, they both tended to disappear. I had no wish to be curious about their relations. I didn't feel left out—on the contrary, I felt that for her these relations were cruelly impersonal. She had to keep advancing, with all the freedom she could command, toward the point she imagined she had seen me looking at, but for her that point was a man like other men, a man who had strayed in among people from whom he was separated by the overly massive certainty, the firmly delimited bodies, which he thrust back, despite himself, into an infinite past. She said to me:

"I feel so strong near him. The strength I have is terrible, monstrous. He can't help but suffer from it. I feel in such good health, it's loathsome, isn't it?"

It was true that, perhaps only in contrast to how little life he had, we felt endowed with an enhanced existence, we felt augmented by ourselves, augmented by what we could be— yes, stronger, more dangerous, more wicked, and in the proximity of a very powerful dream. I felt that. I also felt the danger of this increase in strength, which was in us only because we were close to that immense weakness, and which was perhaps not really in us, but remained outside us like a perverse thought, a will to dominate, a superiority that came to us in a dream and lifted us toward peaks of life, at the very moment when everything seemed to be going as badly as possible as far as the future was concerned. And yet I left the two of them alone. While she disappeared into her alcove, I played. I hid behind the game, deliberately forgetting what an ordeal this intimate, solitary conversation exposed her to. I'm not sure she didn't reproach me for it inwardly, and perhaps what she said to me, suddenly, for no reason—"I have the feeling I will die in a fit of crazy anger against you"—was meant to show me how she had been wounded. She also said to me:

"I dreamed I was tied to a stake on a sort of savannah. Under me, under a thin layer of grass, there was a pit I could vaguely see, probably through a crack, if I bent down. It's a trap, I said to myself, a pit for catching animals. Looking at that pit more carefully, I had the feeling someone was already in it, someone motionless, peculiarly immobile and silent in a way that made me think of you at that point. So you had already fallen into the trap? What were you doing there? I was both pleased and worried. I called out to you, softly, because it must have been dangerous to make noise; then, since you didn't hear, I called a little louder, a little more often, though in a way that still seemed to me very quiet, but it was probably too loud, it must have attracted something threatening whose motions I began to notice, not far from there but behind me, and the fact that it was impossible for me to turn around to see what was coming, since I was tied up, made me angry as well as distressed, but I was also terribly distressed."

Anger and fear. And yet, when she told me the dream, it was with joy, with the pleasure of having dreamed it, she who until then had hardly dreamed at all, only in formless, story-less images which were gone when she awoke.

"Maybe I've learned how to dream now."

This was how she entered the adult phase of the danger. I can't deny that the interest she showed in him touched me, troubled me, exhilarated me, then wounded me. When she said I had pushed her toward him, it was probably true, but it also wasn't true; he himself had drawn her through me, he had beckoned to her, not without my knowledge, but nevertheless without any agreement on my part. From my very first days with her, I was struck by her capacity for merciless feelings. In disgust, she would push away someone who was undergoing a difficult death. There was even a point in the illness beyond which her friendship would come to an end; she said that when things began to go badly for her, she would shut her door on everyone.

"Me, too?"

"You, too, you first."

So it wasn't pity that tied her to him, nor the desire to help him, to be useful to him in that species of remoteness where it seemed possible that he was asking for help simply because he didn't ask for, or give, anything. I said to her:

"He's at death's door. He's in terribly bad shape. Isn't that unpleasant for you?"

"Yes."

The frankness of that *yes* should have kept me from going any farther. So he horrified her. Why didn't she stop seeing him? Why did she involve herself with him so?

"I see very little of him."

But she certainly knew she had a relationship with him the others didn't have, he came downstairs only for her, he no longer spoke to anyone but her, didn't she realize this?

"I don't know. When you question me like that, I can't answer you."

"Please," I said to her. "You've always been perceptive, you've always been able to see yourself clearly. You don't want to start trying to deceive yourself."

She was standing in front of me and I was on my feet too.

A sort of coldness was rising in her like the silent anger whose motions I had already discovered when I had happened to treat her with some indifference. She noticed it right away: the slightest erosion of my desire to see her transformed her into a closed presence which was hard to hold on to. But this time it was the coldness of thought I sensed rising up into these words, which she spoke very fast, with a shiver of familiarity:

"I have no relation of any kind with him. That should occupy me completely."

"Well," I said to her, "how are we going to get ourselves out of this now?"

But she remained convinced that I was the one he would have liked to become friends with. The word she used was not *friendship*, or she tossed it back to me if I lightly said to her:

"He's your friend."

"He would like to be yours. You're the one he's thinking about."

During a brief period, I might have shared that feeling. No doubt when he saw me again, after my return and after he began coming out of his room again (to everyone's surprise—it had seemed that he was finished), I could only attribute to his great politeness the concern he had shown for acknowledging me. As to a convalescent—and he clearly wasn't a convalescent yet—everything could only seem hazy to him, people were shadows, speech a din falling on his ears. What could we have said to each other? And what was he to me? "The professor." What I had retained of him was the nickname she had given him, a name that seemed quite foreign to him, who was so far from indulging in scholarly speech, and yet it seemed correct too: he was worn out—by time, or by the ordeal of an unknown happiness, an unknown torment?—just as one who knows things may be worn out by knowledge. I suspected him of having no memory of himself, almost no thought, as though, in order to avoid the suffering he experienced in any sort of reflection, he had succeeded in remaining a little withdrawn, only admitting the rare images that we chanced to give him and that he gently elevated in us, cautiously and yet with an inflexible motion, into a hard truth about ourselves. But this didn't establish any connection between him and us, still less between him and me. The feeling that he wasn't looking at anyone in particular, that his eyes, so clear, so pale, of a silvery gray, distinguished no one in us but us, and, in us, the most distant part of ourselves, only came to me later as a reassuring image, and it may be that it was quite the opposite. I have reason to believe that he saw only one of us, not all of us as one, but a single being from whom he perhaps expected a little friendship, in fact, perhaps a more immediate sort of help, perhaps nothing but the admission, the unreserved admission that would put an end to everything.

Friend: I wasn't born for that role, I think a different one was set aside for me, one I can't recognize yet. That of giving him a name? Of sustaining him and myself as that name draws near? I can't believe this; it is only a reflection giving a momentary color to the windowpane on which it plays. The name itself separates us, as though it were a stone thrown at him over and over in order to reach him where he is, a stone he perhaps already sensed drawing near through ages and ages. Is that the gesture of a friend? Is that friendship? Is that what he asked me to be—a stone for him, forcing him to recognize himself by such a name, drawing him to it as into a trap? Perhaps in order to catch him in it alive? But who am I, in that case? Who watches with me, near me, as though under a different sky? And if he is what I know of him, am I not entirely abandoned by myself?

Then what is leading him astray? What is he looking for, near me? What has attracted him—what she is to me? The "we" that holds us together and in which we are neither one nor the other? Something too strong for a man, too great a happiness, one of which we know nothing? Maybe it becomes possible for him to breathe near a man who is very happy, maybe he is the breath that mingles with desire, maybe he passes through the moment that disrupts relations and confuses time? Maybe he is behind each one of us, the person we see when the end comes, he who feeds on the time of peace and perfect repose that comes to us then, that he steals away from us—no, that we freely grant him, because he is too much alone, the most unfortunate and poorest of men? But perhaps he is only me, from the very beginning me without me, a relationship I don't want to embark upon, that I push away and that pushes me away.

I also try to convince myself that there was a brief period, shortly after my return, shortly after his, when I saw him as he was, under the cloak of my inattentiveness, and as though in the present, like the others, only a little separated from them by his desire to be forgotten, by his surprise at seeing himself there and knowing it. At that time he talked to me more directly. He seemed to be putting into me certain reference marks: phrases I didn't pay attention to, phrases that remained separate, isolated, strangely sterile, and because of that, cold and motionless, as though he had tried to sow me with seeds from his own memory that might allow him to recall himself at the moment when he would need to come together in himself.

Motionless words I feel now, because of that immobility, an immobility which warns me of something, and makes them heavy, light? Too light for someone who can't let them come to themselves, but instead can only stare at them, without the living space in which they would become animate. He doesn't ask me anything, he doesn't know if I'm there, or if I can hear him, he knows all things, except the *me* that I am, that he only sees and distinguishes through the surprise of his constant arrival: a blind god, perhaps. I don't know myself, I don't know him, this is why he talks to me, he puts forth his words among many others that only say what we say, within the double ignorance that preserves us, with a very light fumbling that makes his presence, which is so very sure, so doubtful. Maybe all he is doing is repeating me. Maybe I'm the one who confirms him in advance. Maybe this dialogue is the periodic return of words seeking one another, endlessly calling out to one another, and only meeting once. Maybe neither of us is there, and she is the only one who holds the secret of that absence, a secret she hides from us.

Naked words to which I am consigned by ignorance. It would be naive to think they gave me control over him. At a certain moment he deposited them in me, probably in many others as well, and this monstrous memory is what we have to carry, together, until the transformation from which we will be delivered only by an end I cannot mistake for an easy death. It is as though he had hidden his life—the hope which mysteriously continued to accompany his life—in one of these words: only one counts, only one is alive, it is surely a word one is not contemplating.

When I think of him, I know I'm not yet thinking of him. Expectation, proximity and the distance of expectation, growth that makes us less, manifestness that caresses itself in us and in us also caresses illusion.

Not absent: surrounded by absence, surrounding us by the feeling of his absence.

It is hard to know if we are not sparing something of ourselves in him. And if he were our hope? If he were what remained of us? What a strange feeling that he might still need us. What a mysterious obligation to have to help him without knowing it and by movements unknown to us, perhaps help him to stay in his place by staying firmly in ours without ceasing to be what we would be without him. Not to question ourselves too much, to avoid the question he asks us about himself, to avoid the dangerous, anxious, shamming curiosity about ourselves that he also gives us. It would be too easy to exclude him or to exclude ourselves. The need to struggle against the feeling he gives me that he is changing me. He's not changing me! He isn't changing me yet!

My embarrassment confronting him, however. If, despite his discretion, he burdened me so much, it was perhaps that his presence lacked all future and all the great future I had imagined he should have represented to us. He was present in such a strange way: so completely and so incompletely. When he was there, I could not help coming up against his self-effacement, which made his approach even heavier, cruelly disproportionate: maybe insignificant, maybe dominating. As though his presence was all there was of him and did not allow him to be present: it was an immense presence, and even he did not seem able to fill it, as though he had disappeared into it and been absorbed by it slowly, endlessly—a presence without anyone, perhaps? But everything made it my duty not to doubt that he was there: more alone, it was true, than I could conceive; pressed, by his withdrawal, against the invisible line which my glances and my thoughts were incapable of approaching, since they couldn't go beyond it.

His presence and not the idea of his presence. It seemed to me this presence destroyed all notion of itself, that I couldn't even have a false notion of it. This was why it was so sure, smoothly certain, a surface that lacked the harshness and roughness I would rather have come up against.

Maybe I saw him without imagining I saw him. Whence the certainty, but almost shorn of the feeling and the illusion of certainty.

Burgeoning of something in him developing in all directions. I felt this: a silent burgeoning, an immediate and excessive thrust toward the inside, the outside. But I felt no less strongly that when he was there, he was there only, entirely, and nowhere else, as though in a place which, because of this exclusive affirmation, was one with him. I believe I had never been able to think he was absent, and if, when I imagined she could have gone to see him in his room, I experienced such a feeling of denial, it was because this was perhaps the only place where I had to believe he was a little absent. That he might have been there, alone, in pain, maybe dying—I could not face that idea, and still less could I suppose that she might be able to cross that boundary of repulsion and really do what I couldn't imagine could be done. There was nothing fantastic in that: on the contrary, there was some sort of hard simplicity, a bareness without fantasy, the rejection of everything that could flatter the imagination, and even anguish; an anguish without anguish, a decision too poor and simple to be approached, the approach of what has no approach. A being that was no longer in any way imaginary, that was unimaginable—this was what I was most afraid of seeing loom up next to me, at my limit.

The most anguishing idea: he can't die, because he has no future.

An idea which concerned me directly, as I realized right away; I was responsible for it and at a certain moment I would have to do something about it, but it also seemed premature to me. However, I didn't forget it. It stayed there, unused, its point always turned toward me.

His solitude, the solitude of someone who no longer has

room to be wrong about himself. He can no longer do more than suffer himself, but this was a suffering he could not suffer. And maybe that was the reason why he tried to endure it in us, in the very thought of us, a thought he tried very hard to turn back to, to come back to, with a movement that was frightened, uncertain, frightened, a movement I felt would not really be carried through. He was there, entirely there, and yet someone who was less himself, who gave less certainty of being himself, someone absolutely insufficient, without reliance on himself or on anything else, without even that fullness of suffering visible on certain faces when for one instant, through some unknown grace of being, the greatest suffering is contained and endured. Then why did he impose himself to such an extent? How was he present, with that simple, evident presence, near us, but in some sense without us, without our world, maybe without any world? And this certainty that something frightful was growing in all directions inside him, especially behind him, with a growth that did not lessen his weakness, a growth from limitless weakness. Why hadn't I been spared such an encounter?

An odd pain, as soon as I tried to picture him in that room, and I knew that if my thoughts deflected me from that room, it was because all he was doing there was dying. A pain that was perhaps only in my thoughts, painful thoughts that made me think by the pressure of some unknown suffering, always the same weight, always the same limit not passed. Is he waiting? Does he know that he's dying and that a person who is dying is always in touch with an infinite future? Tender, gentle weight, patience in which he presses against himself, traversed by himself, silent immobility in which I too have a part—and all of a sudden the feeling that he is turning around, that the immobility in him is turning around, a vision so pressing and so insistent that I couldn't doubt that it corresponded to a real movement, as though, at that moment, he was tempted by the illusion of a circle, coming back toward us as toward his real future, so that once again he could hope to die in advance of himself. And why did I have to resist this movement with all my strength? Why experience it as a threat directed at me? Was it because of the heaviness of my own life, or in apprehension of a greater danger? The agitation of all immobility, all my relations changed for a moment, something brusque, violent, imperceptible, which, even if not accomplished, is accomplished, so that instead of being inside a sphere—enclosed, protected—I form its surface, a finite and perhaps limitless surface. A vision that filled me with surprise: terror and delight. Could I have been even more outside him than he was outside me? Would I embrace him by the limit I would have to form around him, a limit that would wrap him around, grasp him tightly, and, if I held fast, end by enclosing him? The consequence is dizzying. Too dizzying. This turning inside out, once it has been accomplished, allows the balance to be restored, leaves me only with the dangerous impression that, far from bringing me back to some center, my possibility of feeling and seeing is spread out in a circle, being a surprisingly thin, rapid or motionless layer of light revolving around space, unless space itself is performing a sort of revolution.

I continued to feel that I was his limit, then, but it was a very partial limit, an infinitesimal portion that labored obscurely at bounding him on all sides.

The need not to let him separate himself from us. He must not consider us as though we weren't really there. At times like that, it seemed to me we had an urgent obligation to make him feel our proximity, the life in us, the inexhaustible force of life. And, also, not to doubt his right to be there, familiar, barely noticed, friendly. But what was often strongest was the thought that in him we had been dead for a long time: not in that exact form, which would have been almost easy to accept, but in the reflection I read with uncertainty, with resentment, on our faces, that at that point we too had allowed something to die in us that should have found support in us, something that was not only ourselves, but our future and the future of all men and also the last man. A thought that did not yet allow itself to be thought.

The temptation to allow ourselves to disappear, before his gaze, and be reborn as a nameless and faceless power. I sensed that power, I observed that force of attraction, I saw the signs of the strangeness which was attempting to replace us and yet to which we were still attributing a human aspect. Perhaps it was the space between us and him that seemed to me to be filled with a being without destiny or truth, a vague existence and yet a living thing, always capable of coming to life in us and changing us into completely different beings, only like ourselves. I was afraid of being no more than like myself, now, and, even more, of having, both for her sake and my own, the force and the doubt of the distant gaze he had turned in our direction.

A distance that was both fragmented and compact: something terrible without terror, a cold and dry animation, a rarefied, entangled, and mobile life which was perhaps everywhere, as though in that place separation itself had assumed life and force, by obliging us to see ourselves only as distant and already separated from ourselves. The cries, there, the aridity both of the silence and of words, the relentless moans one heard without taking any notice, moans that did not want to be heard. This grew without increasing, a creature whose life seemed to consist in expanding by becoming rarefied, in developing by becoming exhausted, in invisibly breaking off relations by leaving them as they were. And the feeling that we were deceiving ourselves by vainly misleading ourselves, with a falseness that was not real falseness, as though we only wore the aspect of what we seemed to be. A movement of separation, but also of attraction, which seemed to cause faces to become attractive, attracted to one another as though to form, together, the future of a completely different figure, necessary and yet impossible to represent. Nevertheless, his presence. I won't say I remembered him. One can't remember someone who is only present. But, though it sometimes didn't seem that way to me, I didn't forget him either: forgetting has no hold on presence.

Perhaps we never ceased to observe each other. Standing over there, next to the window, and watching—but is he watching, and if he is, where is his gaze going?—he can sense my approach, vague as it is, intense, my impatience, my secret entreaty, just as I can sense his coldness, his resolute limit. At one time, I had been afraid of not proving equal to him or simply of disappointing him by opposing to him a man whose mind he would pass through without noticing or leaving any traces. But now: he slides along, motionless, attracting me by my own effort, provoking me in my certainty in order to prevent it from turning around. When I glimpse him this way, he is different from what I had expected to see of him: younger, with a youthful, questioning expression, in particular, that seems to mask his real face. The feelings I attribute to him are in some sense detached from his face, beyond his features, merely toying with them, and this may be why the suffering I perceive through a momentary contact with him is a second or third face that gives him this appearance of being real only at a distance I don't want to cross. In a palpable way, I am stopped by this suffering, and when I talk to him, I am doing nothing else but trying to keep myself away from it. At least I have not deceived myself about the extreme easiness of his presence. He is manifestly closer to me than I am to him. It is as though I am still interposing myself between us by a lack of attention that fails to create the necessary transparence. As though I become attentive, and I sense that I will respond more obviously to his expectation. When I talk to him, if certain of my words participate in the sort of attention I myself am not capable of, I clearly see that something could happen: that this suffering, or what I call suffering, instead of remaining apart from him and, at the very most, on the surface of his face, could turn around and penetrate him and perhaps fill his great emptiness, a prospect at which I feel a dread that immediately stops everything short.

Aside from these passing moments of irritation, he is extremely tranquil. He is perhaps an entirely superficial man. Hence the resemblance he has to what he is and also the air of simplicity I sometimes discover in him. What she said to me one day: that one might be able to hurt him, but that one couldn't hurt him—and this innocent hurt had seemed to me slighter, more innocuous. But mightn't that hurt beyond hurt be the worst kind? Mightn't that be what gave him the air of simplicity one had to escape? Wasn't that what I had to protect myself from, by feeling that I was remembering it, that I was present, but in a memory? It was present, and yet past, and it was not just any present, but eternal and yet past.

I often heard this warning: "Where you are, you ought to conduct yourself with all the more truthfulness, with an especially pure concern for right conduct because you believe, perhaps wrongly, that you have lost all connection with any true affirmation. Maybe you are only in a middle area, where you call by the name of imposture what you can't look at. Maybe you are still only at the surface and you should go much farther down, but that requires . . . that demands . . . " "No, don't require me . . . don't demand of me . . . "

It may be that she was trying to assuage in me a knowledge that she didn't share, that she didn't reject either, but with which she did not really feel connected. I myself didn't feel connected with my way of looking at things, and still less did I want to subject her to it. Nor did I follow her blindly in all that she seemed to be trying to do or to have me do. I often thought she was losing her way, that the relations forming between them exposed her to a deceptive motion whose insinuation I had felt and from which I could not hope that she would be preserved. I felt it even at the beginning, when he would talk in a bookish way, recounting events from his life that were borrowed and precise, too precise, as though he wanted to leave behind some proof of himself. What he liked to talk about was the city where he was born, a large city apparently located in the East, an impressive city with structures that he described in minute detail, as though to build them before us, with a passion that I expected would reveal something extraordinary to us. But these were only houses like our houses, and he interested himself in these houses with the surprise of someone who has discovered them in his very own words. And yet I was struck by the strange nature of this city, with the broad, dry river that ran through it, with the streets he walked along in the midst of a tumultuous crowd of people on foot constantly moving: there was, he said, a heavy traffic, a coming and going that did not die down at night, as though every single person were always outside, drawn by the pleasure of circulating without hindrance, of being part of a crowd and then losing himself in an even larger crowd. He became exhilarated at this memory.

"It must have been very noisy?"

"Not noisy, but a deep, low, sort of underground murmur, almost calm. Yes, wonderfully calm." He tried to draw us into that city by raising it around us with the images of it we already possessed. He drew us there, but gently, showed it to us in such a way that we, dwellers in large cities and large countries, recognized it more or less as our own: the most familiar one we could imagine and yet, at least for me, completely imaginary, terribly unreal, atrociously doubtful, constructed by him only in order to conceal his own unreality, to give him, among us, a native land, a beautiful horizon of stone and a beautiful smoky sky. Worse than strange: familiar and deceptive and falsifying—or not exactly falsifying, but taking away their basis, their foundation—the pictures of the world closest to us. At first this caused me only a little uneasiness, a slight irritation, but nevertheless something more than any suffering—a serious wrong, the consciousness, right next to my memories, of a proximity of weakness and swooning overtaking me: yes, as though I had had, for a neighbor, a profound but always wakeful fainting fit that had remembered me in order to uproot me from myself. A suffering that exerted itself against my person all the more because a strong feeling—was that what it was, friendship?—prevented me from saying anything that could cause him any difficulty. On the contrary, I never failed to go to his rescue as soon as a question risked reaching him. And perhaps it was this suffering, the need to take responsibility for him, not to exile him by driving him away from such an image of ourselves, that also gave me the feeling we were the ones talking about all that, the city, the visit, and he was the one listening to us talk about it, in that passionate way in which he gave us credit for our efforts.

I was convinced that she entered more seriously than the rest of us into the space where, perhaps under the veil of our own words, we gathered before him. She had left a large city a longer time ago and at a younger age than any of us. She had only a very distant recollection of the noisy world in which, as a little girl, she was inundated with a wonderfully festive power, movie theaters where the darkness was more alive than the pictures, and above all the beauty of the crowds, the immensely upright, erect force of the stone surfaces that created the august essence of the street through which flowed an elusive and inhuman life, as attractive as the life of shadows. She therefore had to go farther back in herself to find the images she needed, and those images, less fixed, closer to their sources than ours, seemed to lead her even farther: over there, as though into another past where we went more quickly, where it seemed that, side by side, we crept more furtively . . . toward what place? Why such haste? But if I questioned her, I saw clearly that for her, this space, which was not veiled by memories, turned out to be as close as possible to her truth, containing no invention, no misrepresentation, and perhaps even without her being aware of it: no, she did not reflect, did not imagine, on the contrary avoided all imaginary reveries, detesting with a kind of rage the poverty of men who try to deceive themselves by wretchedly inventing marvelous things.

Was it out of the same instinct for truth? Was it out of anguish? When I tried to question her, I also noticed how determined she was that the place where we lived should be unassailable. For her, it was a secure base. She trusted it. She did not leave it to go down to the neighboring village. Sometimes, during our walks, we would go to the mountain, where we could see the sea, very far away, like a narrow horizon lifting into the sky and merging with it. This confidence did not mean she had the sort of blind faith in our way of life that almost everyone here shared. She was free of such illusions, she did not believe she would ever leave this place, maybe she didn't want to, maybe she wanted to gather everything she had in the way of belief and certainty inside this narrow circle, beyond it there was nothing but the pale figures of her parents, her sister, who lived in the world as though she belonged there. She was thus joined to this place by an almost frightening sort of understanding. Every sort of connection we have with the vast world, the life that even an entire universe can't contain, she had concentrated in this one place, which was for her firmer, more solid than cities and nations, more diverse, also, and in fact larger because of those empty places opened up at a deeper or shallower level when one or another died here. Well might she be called the queen of the place or given other titles she was naively proud of. I was the only one who didn't like her in the role they made her play, the only one to tell her that, and tell her that I liked her because of her freedom, because she was young and alive, that I would take her away from this place, that she was not committed to it as though it were a convent. Didn't she want to leave? Didn't she want to see other things, real streets, crowds of people?

"Yes," she said, "lots of people." But she added: "You have only seen me here. How do you know whether you would like me somewhere else?" And she went on: "Perhaps you're wrong to say these things to me. It is because of dreams like that that people get lost here."

"And what about me?"

"I don't know about you. I think I'll stop you from leaving, I'll keep you here as long as I have to."

It was perhaps only after some time that I realized how solidly real things were for her, the circle of things, the big central building where we lived, the annexes with their technical apparatus, the little park, the sound of the fountains, each room, the corridor always lit by a white light, the footsteps crushing the gravel outside, the voices of the professionals, the indeterminate and humble voices of the flock, and even the air we breathed, that peculiar, sharp, light air that was also perfidious, like a force seeking to burn joyously the ignored particles of life in us. I won't say this world was more secure when she was there—it was more natural, more closed, like a circle gathering itself more and more into its center, into the dim point that was its center. Where she stood, everything was bright, had a transparent brightness, and of course that brightness propagated itself well beyond her. When one left the room, it was still just as tranquilly bright; the hallway was not about to disintegrate beneath one's feet, the walls remained firm and white, the living did not die, the dead did not come back to life, and farther off it was the same, it was still just as bright, perhaps less tranquil, or perhaps the opposite, of a calm that was deeper, broader— the difference was imperceptible. Imperceptible also, as one walked, was the veil of shadow that passed through the light, but there were already odd irregularities, certain places that were folded back into the darkness, devoid of human warmth, unfrequentable, whereas right next to them shone joyous sunlit surfaces. In the park, for example, stood a chapel no one liked to go into. The faithful preferred to attend the village church. One day, I had gone into this chapel with her, and she had looked at it apparently without any uneasiness, but with great surprise, and the astonishment that invaded and enveloped her would have made her fall, if I hadn't taken her back outside. Was it the cold, the recollection of the things associated with death, even though in other cases these things hardly bothered her? She offered this reason: it was in some sense imaginary, one couldn't help feeling bad there. Even for her, then, there were places where she was no longer as secure and felt dangerously distanced from herself. And even farther away? Where the open country lay, where there was no more circle, where the streets, the houses were scattered about in an autumn fog, where the darkness was like a worn-out day? Farther than the village, the mountain, the horizon of the sea?

I sometimes thought he felt attracted to her because of the security she could guarantee him. The spot where he liked to meet with her, in the alcove near the piano, was no longer merely an abode for pictures and a land of memories, but really a solid little island, a cell just the size for them, tightly enough closed to avoid the terrible pressure of the empty universe and vanished time. This was what made their meeting so anguishing for me, more secret than any other. As though they had enclosed themselves in an inviolable moment, a moment belonging only to them, a sort of standing sarcophagus whose upper wall was her life, her body, which I saw sculpted there with its living reliefs and which arrested the dangerous thrust of our own lives. She was there, like a calm guardian, looking after, watching over the emptiness, scrupulously closing the ways out, a door, a beautiful stone door that protected us from his weakness and protected him from our strength. Guardian, what are you guarding? You who watch, what are you watching over? Who has established you in this place? And yet, I have to admit it: when I looked at them, what struck me was what could reasonably be called their sweetness, their double childlike truthfulness. Perhaps it was this lightness that isolated them from us, a lightness that she did not take directly from herself, but received from him, as I observed without bitterness but with the feeling that this was how he attracted her and connected himself to her, by a bond so light that she saw only the absence of a bond, not noticing that now he spoke only to her and looked only at her. She said, on the contrary, that he did not look at her often, and never directly, but a little sideways—"Toward you, I feel it"—and in fact, once or twice, I had thought I had perhaps caught a tired gaze seeking me out, but this was a gaze which, once it had found you, did not let you go, perhaps because of its fatigue or simply because it was not looking at you. I might ask her: "Doesn't it bother you when he looks at you?"

"No, I like his eyes, maybe they're the most beautiful thing about him."

I cried out: "You find him beautiful?" A question she thought about, with the concern for exactness that she rarely abandoned.

"I could find him beautiful."

"But he's horrifying, he has the face of an old child, not even old, ageless, atrociously expressionless, and his ridiculous pince-nez!" She listened to me with a reproving gravity:

"He doesn't always wear it. He can hardly see clearly anymore, you know. When he wipes it with his cautious gesture, one can see how he trembles, but he hides it, he doesn't want anyone to think he's so sick."

"You're sorry for him. The truth is, you pity him. It's because he seems so unhappy that you're interested in him." She answered indignantly:

"But he isn't unhappy at all. How can you say that? I don't pity him, he doesn't need pity."

"Does that mean he's happy?"

"No, perhaps he isn't happy either. Why are you asking such questions?" I asked her again:

"Well, do you think he's beautiful?"

"Yes, I find him very beautiful, sometimes extraordinarily beautiful." And she added: "His smile is wonderful."

"He smiles?"

Yes, he smiled, but you had to be very close to him to notice it, "a slight smile, which certainly isn't meant for me: maybe it's his way of looking."

When she talked to me like this—and in the beginning, it was rare, but later much more frequent, because of my obstinacy and what seemed to be a need that forced me to turn her thoughts on him in a way that was almost implacable and made her suffer, made her say: "Don't ask me any more questions; at least, not now; let me get my strength back"—I experienced the disturbance I have already mentioned, a sort of exhilaration, of mysterious gratitude, almost of drunkenness, but also a wound: not from the fact that I had to share her interest—that was fair, she wasn't frustrating me at all—but that, because of him, I was entering into a relationship with her that was almost too large, a relationship in which I was afraid of losing her, of losing myself, one I was aware of as an infinite distance separating me not only from her, but from myself, and giving me the impression of distancing us from each other at the same time as it brought us together, allowed us to be together as though through times that were richer, more diverse, but also more uncertain, a labyrinth of time where, if I could have turned around, I would have sensed that another woman was already separating me from her, and from me another man, a disjuncture that perhaps only wanted to scatter us joyously into the sphere of happy immensity, but that I tried to hold back because of a feeling of doubt. For this reason I redoubled my thinking and watching. I don't mean I watched her; rather, I followed her,

I tried to understand the things she did, understand where we were going together, this way, and whether we were already two shadows for each other, joined in the intimacy of the shadow that can no longer be divided by forgetfulness.

In truth, what tormented us most was the feeling that he was so much at risk that there was no room left for anything but waiting. More than once, already, he seemed to have gone beyond the perimeters of what could have been expected. He should have stayed in his room, no longer left his bed, in his bed he should have remained motionless. If he still avoided these precautions, it was not simply out of imprudence, it was not a proof of strength either, in any case not his own strength: one could have imagined that he was using the force of his illness, but that would only have been a play on words. He was still there, but all the same less and less there, with an augmented degree of uncertainty. Over and over again, he would not go out for several days, and once, much longer. I thought we wouldn't see him again. She did not appear any more worried than she had been, and when he was away the longest, she even became almost perfectly calm once again. I was the one who gave evidence of being agitated. I said to myself: could it be possible that she is beginning to forget him? And even though she undoubtedly remembered him, looked at his door when she went by, answered my questions, it was as though this were only a transitory friendship. I asked her: "Aren't you worried?"

"No. Why?" And I didn't always dare say it to her more clearly. I also thought she was getting news about him from the staff. I didn't suspect her of going into his room, even though we were accustomed to visiting certain people, but he was so isolated that he had to be an exception to that. His room seemed to me like a foreign enclave we had no right to inspect, and were we close enough friends with him to go in without being invited? I pictured to myself, I refused to picture, how very weak he became when he was alone. I had always felt that we shouldn't have abandoned him to that solitude: not for an instant, and especially not at night. I was sure he didn't sleep, and I, who slept very little, had a minutely detailed awareness of his nights, a vigilant concern, the feeling that, at least from a distance, beyond the space that separated us, I had to keep watch with him, keep watch over him. One day, when I mentioned his nightly solitude, she made this surprising remark to me:

"But perhaps he is quite cheerful when he's alone."

She was determined to use that word, and said—which for a moment seemed extraordinarily correct to me—that he was the most cheerful person she had ever met, that he had a kind of gaiety she could not always sustain, and I understood why she also sometimes seemed almost cheerful, though it wasn't real gaiety, she only wore a reflection of it, all the more evident because it endowed her with the brilliance of a piece of finery, the sparkle of a precious material which attracted one, perhaps because one wanted to take it off her.

As the days passed, and the feeling that this time he wouldn't get up again became a suspicion that fed on each moment, I was overcome by a terrible desire: I wanted to ask him questions. He couldn't die this way. It wasn't possible that this opportunity would be lost forever, that the irreparable was happening, perhaps at this very moment, at this exact moment. I lost all sense of the existence of limits when I thought he might slip away from me. I wasn't really curious about him. What I wanted had nothing to do with information, it was much more ephemeral. Maybe my desire was merely the quite human desire to get close to him. Could one leave him to himself? And if he did actually turn to me, it could only make me sad that I hadn't understood the simple truth of that movement. But it was especially when I saw her so tranquil, her spirit and life almost obliterated, that I suddenly sensed to what an extent I had left it all in her hands, with a lazy confidence that had made it easy for me to wait. I had stolen away. The only reason I had admired her, in all her naturalness, was so that I could remain at a distance. And no doubt it was really true that she had been wonderful, she had behaved as no one else could have behaved, and it was also true that he was happy with her and only with her. But that didn't mean I was released from having any relationship with him. And why was she so tranquil? Where did this calm come from, this calm I collided with, as with a space I was moving through feverishly, anxiously? Why didn't I share it at all? Why did I have to be more worried the less she was? Why did she seem to forget him? Why did it happen that what, for her, was forgetfulness crowded into me like a sharp point forcing me to remember?

One night, maybe because I had been sleeping deeply for a long time, I had the feeling that he was in a very bad way. I woke up with that certainty. I must have told her about it in the dim consciousness of just awakening. When she didn't answer, I turned on the lamp. She was sitting almost straight up, bowing her head under the light and hugging her knees, as she liked to do. She was on the very edge of the bed, constrained at that limit by the coercive force of her animosity. To me, the strangest thing was that she was awake like that, like a person who had clearly been awake for some time. When she couldn't sleep, as occasionally happened, she would say to me right away: "I can't sleep," in a small, desperate voice, because the disappearance of sleep seemed to her such an incomprehensible misfortune; she would also say, simply, that there was nothing in the world sadder than to sleep alone, and only a very particular set of circumstances would cause her to spend a whole night in her room, which lay farther down at the bend in the corridor. Of course I said to her:

"What in the world is wrong?"

Her head was still bowed. I was as surprised to see her awake in the middle of the night, this way, as I would have been if I hadn't found her next to me when I woke up, and more frightened. Maybe she had been afraid and had called out to me; since I was sleeping deeply, I hadn't heard her, and she had been overcome by one of those silent rages that closed her in on herself, so that it was only by chance that one could draw her out: by a gesture, a word, a certain kind of attention or even a distraction that affected her without one knowing why or being able to predict it. At that moment I was too agitated to find a way to bring her back to me. All I could think of saying was: "What's the matter? What's the matter?" Words she detested:

"How can I say what the matter is when you ask me with those little words?"

But this time she didn't answer, she contracted visibly, as though to avoid being touched by something horrifying. I asked her if she had had a bad dream, if she had heard a strange noise and, thinking once again of my presentiment, I tried to tell her about the feeling I had had, that he might be in a very bad way, that we ought to find out: "Wasn't she worried? Did she know something?" And I ended by saying something I shouldn't have said, but which had taken shape in me a long time before:

"I would like to talk to him, I would like to see him."

As I said that, I reached out my hand to her and finally

touched her. Her body seemed incredibly hard to me, more so than any truly hard thing could be. Scarcely had I even grazed her than she leaped up, crying out indistinct words which surely expressed an excruciating ignorance and rejection. I didn't have time to study them, I wanted only to get her back, and in fact, she immediately collapsed in my arms, everything in her that was hard melted, became soft, of a dreamlike fluidity, while she wept and wept. I never really knew what had happened to her that night. I couldn't interpret that scene, or understand it, only remember it: she had been overwhelmed, and in effect time had been overwhelmed too, so that I seemed to be witnessing something very ancient or still to come. I dared say to her:

"Maybe you mistook me for him." Which she denied categorically:

"How can you say that?" It almost made her laugh.

"Or someone else?"

"Maybe someone else. No one I know."

"But was it that horrible?"

"No, no."

"Then were you asleep?"

"I don't think so." And seeing that I kept coming back to it, she added, "It's nothing. What are you trying to understand? There's nothing to understand."

But I couldn't help trying to get close to a moment as serious as that, one when I had seen her so far away from me, incapable of recognizing me, of loving me, as though on the edge of the world we shared. And what had she said? Childishly, I convinced myself that if I had heard them more clearly, those words would have enlightened me about her, about myself, about everything else. I questioned her desperately. She answered:

"But I didn't say anything, it was a shout that didn't

mean anything. Maybe I didn't even shout." In the end I wondered if that scene hadn't revealed some kind of deep jealousy on her part. Maybe she was jealous of my interest in him, jealous of what she said was his interest in me. She insisted too much on that preference of his, she kept harking back to it, as to a painful place, without being aware of it, and I hadn't been aware of it either, up to then. That thought, so very human and yet so barely credible to me, touched me, made me as calm as she was. So we had to wait calmly, and even if waiting implied a responsibility that required of us an active adherence, I felt, now, after that night and because of it, that everything was simpler and richer than I could even imagine. I had been struck by what I had said to her—"I would like to talk to him, I would like to see him"—words that had been almost shameful to me, because of the very personal desire they had brought to the surface, words that could well have made her jealous by revealing to her how deep a desire existed, involving only me. And yet those words did not seem out of place to me. There was something timid and irresistible about them that touched me: an adolescent sort of desire that could only have been conveyed here by the whole immensity of universal time. And perhaps this only said something about me, only said what I wanted, but she was the one I was addressing when I said it, this young woman sitting here, as though at my very edge, whom I was touching now, just now, and why had she been so overwhelmed? By a sadness I did not allow for, instead tormenting her with tireless questions, a tireless investigation, that she plaintively rejected, not wanting anything to do with a memory which she wouldn't have been able to resist?

When, not long after that night, I said to her: "For some time now, you have seemed quite calm to me," all she said was:

"But maybe I'm not calm." And then, after some thought, out of her concern to be precise, she added: "There is often something like a point, an extremely fine point, that tries to force me to retreat, tries to push me back into being calm. I can only feel the point, and not the calm at all."

For me, that answer was like the point she was telling me about, whose presence I felt: a suffering so sharp and fine that one couldn't tell whether it was still far away or already absolutely present, though constantly approaching, and too lively for one to be able to control it. I didn't know what was conjured up by that point, that suffering which nailed me in place and yet pushed me hither and thither because of an uneasiness that had all the signs of gaiety. There was something obscure about it that I was turning away from, that I couldn't accept, that probably had to do with him, with the serious condition that was threatening him. However, I wasn't relieved of it when, yet again, he made it through that bad episode, which they discreetly called an attack of the flu: scarcely even more tired than he had been, though each time I was distressed to see how much weaker he was in reality than I remembered—and yet, not only weaker. It was as though an inordinate power had swept down on him and by crushing him so excessively had endowed him in turn with a power— to give it that name—superior to everything, a powerlessness over which, now, no superiority had any hold. (What would happen to a man who came up against a death too strong for him? Every man who escapes violent death wears, for an instant, the glimmer of that new dimension.) So he was back in the same alcove, waiting for her, waiting for us, and I wasn't at all reassured by this proof that he wasn't in a very bad way. On the contrary, the very sharp, fine point only became sharper and finer. I was at the gaming table and he was in the armchair, his large body somewhat hunched over, but in a rather graceful position. I had occasionally seen him leaning forward in that same armchair, his head bowed over his rapidly rising and falling chest, his felt hat casting a shadow that moved over his face. Today, he made a better impression, he also looked healthier. He must have felt that I was examining him. For a moment, he looked in my direction, with at first a very brief look that seemed to fall back on himself, then, when it lifted again in my direction, it grew broader, but far from being the penetrating look I was hoping for, remained vague, though clearly directed at me, but too ample, observing me slowly as though, instead of me, it had to embrace the entire expanse of a great crowd.

While he was looking at me in that disappointing way, I thought I discerned the beginnings of a smile, a little suffering smile, maybe ironic, maybe absent. The effect was immediate and struck me with the promptness of a stab of pain piercing me in the most distant of my memories: pain that was actually his own. It was this, then, that was conjured up by the point, his own pain, the idea that he was suffering in a way that was beyond us, and also beyond him. I won't say that I was only discovering it now. I had thought about it all too much, I had conjured it up, I had denied it, a suffering more terrible than that of a child, entering him so deeply that nothing of him was visible anymore but unlimited weakness and the gentleness that resulted from it. Early on, when he was asked: "Are you suffering?" he always answered: "No." Despite the fact that this "No" was very gentle, very patient, of an almost transparent tenuousness, he was gently rejecting our pain: he was filled with an unknown pain, one that wasn't accompanied by any moaning, that one couldn't question, or pity, a pain brighter than the brightest day. That "No," coming from a man who almost always said "Yes," was terrible. It represented the secret breaking point, it indicated the area beyond which he regarded us, and even our suffering, as no longer existing.

"Why, with his kindness, isn't he willing to say: *Yes, I'm suffering a little*, a speech that would be a sign of alliance? Maybe he can't communicate what he is going through; maybe no one is there to take in what he is suffering."

For this reason, I thought he was dying, but not suffering. In fact, we were afraid of that suffering, which risked surviving him if he didn't suffer it all the way through. I didn't dare say to myself what I nevertheless read on his face and what she made me deal with by answering me in a sort of horrified way:

"How can you say he isn't suffering? When he thinks, he suffers, and when he doesn't think, his suffering is naked." And she added with simplicity: "He must be given a little thought that isn't a thought of pain, a little moment, I think that would be enough."

So she tried to procure for him that little bit of time—that single moment that might allow him to recover the pain, to suffer it? A single instant, but a true instant? What a dreadful complicity, what an instinct—and what an abyss it was drawing her to, drawing us to.

Already, when she had gone with him just now—he had withdrawn after a brief period of standing behind the gaming table, he clearly could not tolerate so much noise for long, despite his willingness—seeing them walk past together, though she wasn't touching him, but remained a slightly apart from him in order not to get in his way as he walked, I had felt a pang.

"That's what had to happen."

And the fact that they were hardly together, that she, walking near him, was still quite alone, as though she found herself there by chance, with her own reasons for going away, did not diminish, only increased, the distance by which I felt endangered. Yet she didn't go far. She opened the elevator door for him and held it open while he sat down on the seat inside. I thought they were going up together, but before the whistling of the pulley stopped, she was already back. I wanted to let her take my place. Gambling was a pleasure of hers that she had been trying to inspire in me for a long time, and not only in me, in many others as well. She lavished her gaiety on it, her lightness, her chance, too, she loved that chance and loved being loved by chance. But this time she didn't play. She remained apart, her face closed and motionless, not visibly preoccupied, but distant, prey to a resentment she wouldn't have been able to formulate. I thought uneasily: and what if she stays like this? I recalled the night I had found her awake and yet so horribly withdrawn: the fact that by touching her, I had actually succeeded in touching her, even though at the price of terrifying her—perhaps this was what was so wonderful, perhaps it was a wonder that might not always recur—or that might always recur, always? It was then that I boldly expressed to her the thought that perhaps he was not suffering, and she gave me, with such stinging promptness, the answer which the two of us now confronted. I couldn't hold it against her. I could only hold it against myself that I hadn't done anything up to now to stop her from approaching that area of suffering to which, surely, she turned and turned again, ceaselessly, moving away from it, going back, or maintaining that motionlessness, that calm which I now understood might have yet another, completely different meaning from what I had thought I saw in it: that calm might be similar to the calm one imposes on oneself near people who are very sick and suffering a great deal, in order to spare them any painful vibration, a calm that could not entertain any question about him, any uneasiness, scarcely even a thought. But this did not result in any calm, only a ruder silence and a rough, hard noise, a silence and a noise which, to a terrible degree, lacked any sort of musical quality and made the frequenting of places and people here very difficult. Even the moans, the calls, at night, still had something dry about them that didn't arouse pity, didn't summon anyone, didn't reach anyone, a slow torment, an imperceptible decline that had to be connected with his own suffering, the suffering he consumed in silence and with infinite patience, though in vain—it was there around us, all the heavier because it was so light, pushing us back, moving us away, attracting us, scattering us.

What would happen if he died too soon? If the suffering survived him? And immediately this thought: what if he were already dead? If what I took to be him was only the surviving, silent presence of his suffering, the specter of an infinite pain that would henceforth remain with us, weigh upon us as we lived, worked, endlessly died? An abject thought, born of that suffering, already, of the fatigue of that suffering, of the desire to relieve myself of it and relieve her of it too. It seemed to me she had alluded to it a long time ago, already, in a veiled manner and without my noticing, without my doing anything to deflect her from it, as I recalled only the circumstances of that confidence, circumstances I had liked. One evening she had wanted to go out and walk on the lawn, and as we passed the vast kitchens, which for reasons of hygiene we weren't allow to enter, she had drawn me into the back courtyard. There was already a little snow, but the sky wasn't a snowy sky, and it was here that I saw how dark and confined space could be, as though receding to an infinite distance and yet also coming infinitely close to us.

"Look how dark the sky is."

The cold, and probably the sudden chill of fear—she had always told me she was afraid of going out at night—as well as the constraint I had exerted on her to force her to look at the black sky, had made her dizzy and I had led her over to the rim of the basin that served as a fish pond for the kitchen. We remained there side by side. Everything was quiet and we heard only the noise of the water, a mysterious, living noise in which one sensed the confused agitation of the fish, disturbed by our presence. She soon felt better and wanted to stand up, but once again she felt dizzy, complained of violent pains in her head. Where we were, there was a thicker layer of snow. She said to me:

"I think if I were to put my bare feet in the snow, I would feel better. Help me."

I took off her shoes, unfastened her stockings, and slipped them down, then she sank her feet in the snow which I gathered to her in a little pile. She stayed that way, me with my arms around her legs. She said:

"We shouldn't go back to the house ever again."

"Is that what you want?"

"Yes, right now it is."

"But where would we go?"

"Wherever you like."

The front of the house rose a few steps away, not all of it was visible, it formed a powerful dark mass, its lower stories dimly lit, but everything at the top lost in darkness. I became aware of the change that her words seemed to announce in her. Did this mean she was prepared to abandon everything without any regrets?

"Yes."

"But you've spent your whole life here."

"My whole life, but hardly a life."

I suggested that she might not be able to tolerate it, she had adapted to living in such particular conditions, it would probably be very dangerous.

"Do you mean that I would have a relapse?"

"Yes, maybe."

She thought for a moment:

"I think I could die, but not suffer—no, I can't."

"Are you afraid of suffering?"

She shivered. "I'm not afraid of it, I just can't, I can't."

An answer which at the time only seemed to me to contain a reasonable fear, but perhaps she had meant something quite different, perhaps at that moment she had expressed the reality of the suffering one could not suffer, and perhaps she had thereby revealed one of her most secret thoughts: that she, too, would have been dead a long time ago—so many people had died around her—if, in order to die, one had not had to pass through such a thickness of sufferings that were not fatal and if she had not been terrified of losing her way in an area of pain so dark that she would never find her way out of it. I had not given that speech any real attention, or I had managed not to look at it squarely, but now I grasped it again as I had not been able to hear it before, in her cold, shivering presence, in that silent snowy landscape, under that sky reduced to a single point, while I tightly encircled her legs and her naked thighs, drawing her toward me little by little, so that in the end, as though seized once again by the same dizziness that had shaken her in the beginning, she fell down next to me.

We were still in the library. It occurred to me that we should go back up to the room. That would mean going back up in his direction, walking down the corridor where I had heard him approaching with his hesitant, though sure, step, climbing from very far away and as though he were still very far away, and yet going past, going farther on. I never seriously thought he would enter. I knew he wouldn't stop, and now I knew I would be the one who would go to his room someday. Would I be alone? Yes, I would be alone. And what would ensue from that moment? What could I do? Try to reach him in order to relieve him of himself, in order to give that suffering a face, to draw it from its muteness, force it to express itself, even though it might express itself in the form of a cry that would overpower me? And why go bother him, why force him to recognize in me, because of my approach, the frightful suffering he would otherwise endure in silence? Why talk to him, make that suffering talk? There was something about it that was necessary, but revolting, which I resisted with some unknown part of myself. Everything to do with him was disturbance. There was an area of disturbance around him, a dissolute reality that inspired disgust: around him and maybe in him. It was low, one had to descend too low to reach it, and the only movement that responded to that summons was a movement of abhorrence, the need to lower him still further, to crush him or even merely to touch him, not through any direct violence, but by a slow, cunning attack, commensurate with his dissimulation, and yet to attack him also in the face, that face which he would protect with his great frightened hands, while behind them his fear, his distress, his derision would shine out: yes, crush him, make him even more himself, after which we would be free, there would be an amazing moment of freedom and emptiness through which the force and impetus of an unknown happiness would fly to meet us.

Dreadful daydreams, thoughts that were too much for me and in which I didn't recognize myself. If I must assail him for something, let it be in a friendly spirit, and let my hand alone strike him, my hand and not my thoughts, my thoughts, not my afterthoughts—and let it be without disgust, without knowing it and without wishing it. If I must be his destiny, let that destiny attack him, not degrade him. But I immediately thought: that is even more cowardly, that leaves me the dignity of a tranquil, protected soul. Such a thing can't be, and if it is, it can only be horrible, a repugnant misery, an ugly wound from which no one will recover, something wicked, hideous, sordid, an invasion of vulgar shames and banal resentments. And it won't be just once, but every time, and every time he'll be more degraded, weaker, in greater suffering, and I'll be more powerful, more fanatical, and happier. That's where we're going, that's the truth of this meeting, the propensity of this truth. Does she know that? And if she knows it, what is she thinking, what does she expect? I was able to ask myself the question, but I couldn't answer with certainty. Sometimes she seemed cruel to me, and she was cruel, opinionated, implacable concerning everything she couldn't tolerate. What she rejected, she rejected with violence, loving, not loving. But sometimes she was infinitely resourceful and wonderfully patient: with animals, for instance. It occurred to me that some of the understanding, the friendship she had for him was the sort one has for an animal. Maybe he horrified her, but she accepted him, as she had told me one day when I said to her:

"You don't know who he is."

"No, I don't, but I have accepted him."

Yes, she accepted him—that word said a great deal.

It was in the light of that word that I wanted to open the space between us once again. During the entire evening after the words had sprung from her that ought to have set her free, she had remained just as distant, her face smooth, almost without contour, almost ugly, and even so, I wanted passionately to caress that face, but as soon as I put my hand near her at that moment, however rapidly and gently, she turned her head away or stubbornly bowed it. A dangerous reserve that kept an appearance of vivacity and seemed to model itself on her without altering her behavior, but which, if I complained about it, she saw as merely the reflection of my coldness. It is true that I had not answered her words. I couldn't challenge them, nor could I accept them. I had no doubt that at the point we had reached—and as I could still feel the vibration of their keen shafts in me—it would have required only a little encouragement for her to come to the conclusion I had been waiting for so long: "You must go see him." A speech which, once it had established itself between us, risked separating us for good. Shouldn't I, in turn, conclude from this that she herself had already been to see him, perhaps briefly, perhaps as a familiar visitor? If I had sometimes believed and sometimes wished that she had gone into his room, it was only because I had never imagined it. And how could she have remained silent about such a thing? How could she have carried it around and hidden it behind her thin face? No doubt I hadn't asked her that and hadn't wanted to ask her, but the fact is that there couldn't have been any room for such a question between us.

Then I had to think that maybe she had taken this step, not by taking it, but because she had refused to take it. That was how she had learned things she wouldn't have learned by going all the way, though the natural motion she had ought to have taken her all the way. Likewise, she would always refuse to talk to me about it, and I participated in the same refusal by not questioning her. And yet I felt that if I managed to find an occasion to question her, she would answer me immediately in the frankest way. Everything, therefore, depended on me, on the question.

Nevertheless, to realize how difficult it would be for me to come to that, I had only to recall the night she had remained at such a distance from me, a distance which really seemed to lay down on her the reserve which it wasn't enough for me simply to push away now, which, on the contrary, I had to leave intact, sensing that this was the only place we could henceforth reach each other without reserve and talk to each other without lying. In this sort of interval, I was sure she would not hide anything from me, but only to the extent that I, too, by a difficult agreement, would enter it. Would I ever consent to stop pressing her and searching for her? Certainly I could often reproach myself for the way I had continued to pester her, even in her sleep and even in the calm with which she protected herself. I could sense the element of hopelessness in the sudden horror that had made her leap out of that moment of the night in which I had touched her. Every time I went back over it, I kept finding in myself the wonderful nature of that movement, my sensation of joy in recapturing her, of luminousness in embracing her disorder, feeling her tears, and that her dream body had not been an image, but an intimacy overwhelmed by sobs. A moment so real that it consoled one for everything and exceeded all hope, all sadness, and all thought. That was what I would always remember, as I would recall all the moments we spent together in my room. She would remain on the balcony for hours, lying down, drawing rather childish landscapes or exclusively female figures related to her by a vague resemblance—her sister, she would say, or at other times: "What I am to you."

She wasn't surprised to see me watching her constantly, without any other concern, but without any insistence either. She said my look had little weight, that it made the things around her lighter.

"Is it as though you were alone?"

"No."

"Is it as though I were alone?"

"Not that either: maybe it's your look that is alone."

She rarely lifted her head, there on the other side of the windowpane, wrapped in blankets, while she drew the lines with a hand that moved almost constantly. Her essence, then, seemed to me, not childish, but so divorced from thoughts of the future, so present and yet so scarcely burdened by the present, so gravely, knowingly insouciant, that I could only look at her with a certain drunkenness, and it was no doubt this that gave her, in turn, the feeling of lightness that made her almost drunk, too—yes, in the long run, she was somehow abandoned to a spirit of lightness she wasn't always sure she could control.

"And yet you're calm."

"Yes, I'm calm, but it's already almost like a memory, the most distant sort of memory."

"It's already in the past?"

"Yes, maybe in the past."

But, with her inevitable concern for exactness, she took care to add:

"That point is still there, that extremely fine sort of point which forces us to retreat, to go back into the heart of the calm."

"Us? Me too?"

"Yes, us. Only us."

In fact, it sometimes happened that she couldn't stay where she was: she hastily tosses back the blankets, comes into the room, and her haste, her fever keep her there, in some way motionless, until she finds a way out that leads her to me, but also to other days, as though there had been other days: back there, in the past, in a space where people seem to walk more quickly, glide by, close together, more furtively. What place are they going to? Why such haste? Sometimes they separate and look at each other, as though another memory lay between them, not a memory—forgetfulness, a torment that draws a circle around them and isolates them. She had always been afraid of dying outside herself; she would say:

"You have to hold me firmly. I must be struck at the point where you're holding me."

At a certain moment, she had begun to want to recall something: she searched for it quietly, with a certain uneasiness, but also with great tact and firm patience. If she could have gotten up, she would no doubt have gotten up to look for it in the room and all through the house, as though she were playing a game:

"Here?"

"Or here?"

"No, nowhere near here."

There was an allusion to that forgotten thing in everything she did, an allusion so discreet, so veiled that no one dared take notice of it: it happened a little in the background, behind her and behind him; maybe it concerned both of them. When she died, she gave one the comforting, hopeless feeling that she was dying in order to remember it. Later—it was already the middle of the night—without emerging from her immobility, she asked suddenly:

"Am I the one who's dying? Or is it you?"

Words which he heard distinctly. He leaned over her and she opened her eyes, looking at him with that serious, motionless, solitary look which, it seemed to him, she had now. It was like the reminder of a promise she was asking him to keep.

As we were rising tranquilly, having left the drawing rooms, which were empty of people now, no other noise between us but the whistling of the pulley, as I listened to that noise, which I had noticed before, I thought that, with me, she was finishing the journey she had embarked upon a short time back. She would open the door of the elevator, walk along by my side, but a little behind, not completely level with me, leaving a gap of a few steps between us, as she could not help doing when she was "on bad terms" with me. It would be like that all the way down the famous corridor, a narrow corridor with door after door opening onto it, awash day and night with the same white light, without shadow, without perspective, and crowded, like a hospital corridor, with a ceaseless, muffled din. All the doors were alike, all white, of the same white as the wall, indistinguishable from it, indistinguishable from one another except by the numbers on them, and as one walked down it, everything seemed equally sonorous, equally silent, as in a tunnel—footsteps, voices, murmurs behind doors, sighs, happy slumbering and unhappy slumbering, fits of coughing, the whistling sounds of those who were having trouble breathing, and sometimes the silence of those who did not seem to be breathing anymore at all. I liked that corridor. I walked down it with a sense of its calm, deep, indifferent life, knowing that for me the future was there, and that I would have no other landscape than that clean, white solitude, that there my trees would grow, there would lie the immense, rustling fields, the sea, the changing, cloud-filled sky—there, in that tunnel, the eternity of my encounters and my desires.

Once we were standing before the door, having come to a stop without opening it, I was seized by—what thought? By a thoughtless sadness, one that asked nothing, imposed nothing, could say nothing, could not be consoled, was merely empty, and curtly separated us, as though she were at one end of time and I at the other—but in the same instant and in a shared presence, side by side. Did she understand that this was necessary? She gave the door a quick look, gave me a quick look too, and went off to her own room, which lay farther down at the bend in the corridor.

II

IF I THINK ABOUT what happened, I would have to say that for me it almost merges with the calm that allowed me to face it. This calm was a gripping sort of calm, very close to the word that came from so far away: it wasn't completely commensurate with me, it was even extraordinarily outside of me, but that didn't bother me, I had my own share in it, it touched me, it even pushed me back slightly, as though to keep me on the edge of the moment when I would have to be calm.

I applied my mind to it, and even though there was no real relation between us, I had the impression there was a space to which I felt bound by an expectation, by precautions, doubts, an intimacy, a solitude that would perhaps have been suitable for a living being—a human being? No, it wasn't human yet, it was more exposed, less protected, though more important and more real; but because that space was foreign to me, I did not know what bound me to it. I only knew that I owed it some respect, and I didn't even know that, because perhaps I also owed it a fierce lack of respect.

In addition to that first impression, I also felt that this space, while appearing infinitely distant and foreign, offered me a sort of immediate means of access. It seemed to me that if I managed to be calm, to be equal to that calm, and to be, in myself, what that calm was outside me, I would remain in balance not only with all my thoughts, but with the motionless, grave, and solitary thought under whose cover my thoughts continued to express themselves so lightly.

All I had to do was wait. But waiting . . . Had I made the decisive moves? Didn't I have to be more lively in my study of that event, that very recent event by which I felt I was being watched, by means of which I was undoubtedly watching myself, looking after the calm that was confided to my negligence? And yet, as though despite myself, I was already enjoying this new state. I had never been so free, and except for that grave, motionless thought, my thoughts, too, were freer, lighter, almost too light, yielding me up to a spirit of lightness that threatened not to leave me at my own level for very long. If I had wanted to, I would have thought everything. But I had to beware of precisely that—beware of the even more enticing impression that we thought everything, that every thought was ours.

I won't say that this space was already clearly delimited, but it could have been, I felt that, and a doubt remained that it was delimited as soon as I entered it, at least might have been. The doubt weighed powerfully on each of my steps, not only to push me back, but also to make me go forward. If there hadn't been an uncertainty between it and me that protected both of us, if there hadn't been my weakness, its weakness, my weakness so superior to me, so decided and so sure, I wouldn't even have been able to be conscious of the thought that was vast enough to contain the two of us.

But I did not doubt the kind of presence it constituted. As soon as I was there, I observed it, I experienced it, I leaned lightly on it, my forehead leaning on my forehead, and what held me back was something too easy in that approach, which left it without any defense and me without any decision. It was too simple. This easiness might have been what had deflected me for so long: one gesture and always within my reach. I could only be surprised at it and avoid it.

Something warned me that the doubt should always be equal to the certainty, and the certainty of the same nature as the doubt.

I had to wait, allow it to gain strength from that waiting, affirm itself in its contact with me and exhaust me with that calm. It had to find limits that were not too foreign to mine, nor too strict: it could close up again, but on me. Its instability was what suddenly scared me, and yet I dreaded, just as much, a distinctness that would have brought it too close to me. It would have frightened me more as a familiar thing than as a foreign thing.

Everything was so calm that if it hadn't been for the soft, continuous pressure exerted on me, an extremely light and extremely firm pressure that I wasn't sure I wasn't exerting on it by my resistance and by the direction of my waiting, I could have believed I had already reached some goal—an ultimate one, perhaps, one of the ultimate goals. And yet, the calm also seemed to interpose itself between us, not as an obstacle, true, nor as a distance, but as a memory.

A dangerous calm, I realized once again, and one that was in some sense a danger even to itself, threatened, threatening, yet unshakable, indestructible—it was final, a word which here appeared opaque, but light.

It was dark, it was cold. The waiting (the calm) made me feel that over there, on one of the slopes which I could only situate over there, was an opening onto a different region, one that was even more useless and more hostile and that we both dreaded in the same way.

The space was evasive, wily, frightened. Maybe it had no center, which was why it disoriented me by its evasion, its wiliness, its temptation. It stole away; it kept stealing away, and yet not always. Abruptly, I had before me a hungry evidence, an ultimate avidity which I had to escape, as though it were drawn, in me, by the sense of that center which it didn't have or by that calm that awaited me. A terrible feeling that immediately made me draw back. But I, too, became wily, I learned not to be content with it, not to return to myself. I never despaired, I tirelessly prowled around. I had lost every habit, every path. The only firm thing I had was the motionless thought that enveloped us and perhaps protected us.

And yet, I had glimpsed some possibilities, recognized the places where everything became denser, more real. It was like a slope one had only to follow, a slope that started off from calm and ended in calm. On either side were shining images, an endless din. That din made me drunk, perhaps crazy. It seemed to me motionless, high, and smooth, it was a height that pushed me back down toward the bottom, a speech untouched by the silence. It was at once powerful and empty, authoritarian and docile. It was uttered far away from here, far away even from the space, and as though outside, over there in the useless region, and yet also in me.

A feeling that at no price should I make use of the agitation of that speech, nor adhere to it. But I stayed on the crest of that narrow drunkenness, cramped against a phantom of lightness, controlling a feeling of pain, of joy, not controlling it. It was light, joyous, of an amazing lightness, it allowed itself to be seen rather than heard, a shining sphere, a sphere that merged with its surface, kept growing, and was calm as it grew. The agitation of a speech in no way confused—and when it falls silent, it does not fall silent: I could distinguish myself from it, only hear it while hearing myself in it, this immense speech which always said "We."

The sort of drunkenness that sprang from it came from that "We" which sprang from me and which, far beyond the room where the space began to enclose itself, obliged me to hear myself in that chorus whose base I situated over there, somewhere in the direction of the sea.

That was where we all were, over there, erect in the solitude of our unity, and what we said ceaselessly praised what we were:

"What else is there now but us?"
"No one."
"Who are the distant ones and who are the close ones?"
"We here and we over there."
"And who are the oldest and who the youngest?"
"We are."
"And who must be glorified, who comes to us, who waits for us?"
"We must and we do."
"And the sun—where does it get its light from?"
"From us and only us."
"And the sky—what exactly is it?"
"The solitude that is in us."
"Then who must be loved?"
"I."

A mysterious answer, a strange murmur that disturbs us: the voice is weak, harsh like the squeak of a lizard. Our own has the volume and strength of worlds added onto worlds, but it is also silent. The other has something animal about it, too physical. Almost imperceptible, it shakes us. Even though it may be a sort of ritual, hearing it is a disquieting, sublime surprise.

A feeling of immense happiness—this is what I can't get rid of, what radiates eternally from these days, what began the first moment, what makes that first moment still continue, always continue. We remain together. We live turned toward ourselves as though toward a mountain lifting vertiginously from universe to universe. Never any stop to it, no limit, a drunkenness ever drunker and calmer. *"We"*: the word glorifies itself eternally, rises endlessly, passes between us like a shadow, lies under our eyelids like a gaze that has always seen everything. It is the shelter we hurry under, knowing nothing, our eyes closed, and our mouths are also closed. How we nevertheless see things, that strange sun, that terrible sky—this is what doesn't preoccupy us. Insouciance is the gift we have been given, and from the first moment, it was already a very old thing: the feeling of that altitude, an immense column whose top and bottom, merging, put us within reach of an infinite growth. Yes, it always goes farther. It is always more indestructible, always more immobile: eternity is achieved, but grows on. Such a discovery is accepted right away. No beginning and yet the soar of a perpetual awakening. No end, but an aspiration always satisfied and always desiring. This thought scarcely weighs upon our shoulders, there is nothing solemn or grave about it, it is lightness itself, it makes us laugh, that is our way of examining it. Frivolity is what is best about us. It unsettles us to praise ourselves for being frivolous: as though an unknown center were being touched in us.

Sometimes, the sky changes color. Already black, it becomes blacker. It increases by one tone, as though to show that the impenetrable has withdrawn still further. I could be afraid I am the only one to realize this. Everything, it claims, is common to us, except the sky: our share of solitude passes through this point. But it also says this share is the same for everyone and we are all united within this point even in our separation, united only here and not elsewhere: this would be the ultimate goal. What proves it is that every time the black becomes blacker, by a nuance that can only be communicated within our very midst, what each of us then secretly says, in order to give reality to that sign, rises from all sides into one common cry that alone reveals to us what we have caused ourselves alone to hear. A terrible cry, apparently always the same. What is terrible about it at its highest point does not change, and yet we know that it varies imperceptibly in response to the intangible variation of the sky. That is why it is terrible.

We wouldn't tolerate the sky being a single point. This is probably the source of the thought that has lain down on me, that wraps me around and protects me like a veil:

"But if it weren't a point, if it weren't as infinitesimal as the sharpest needle point, how could I bear it? Do you mean the sky sinks into us like the point of a needle?"

"That's it, yes, that's right."

This point would therefore be what pierces the most distant of my memories. The greatest calm reigns. It's a unique moment. Certainly, here we are attaining something that was not hoped for, that comes unexpectedly, that happens the very moment we expected the opposite: one gets up (if one was lying down); one freezes, if one was running (perhaps one was running away); or, to put it better, one stops and bows one's head as though to reflect. True, I don't remember this. Speech informs us about it, image shows it to us, memory does not encounter it: we move about uselessly behind ourselves. And yet, I remember many things—everything, maybe, but not that moment, and as soon as I move toward it more boldly, I run up against that extremely fine and amazingly distant point: that black point we call the sky, that single changing point, ever blacker and sharper, which we find suddenly before us and which is there only to urge us to withdraw, go back inside the calm from which our lightness has also eternally made us go forth.

What, then, would remove us from the calm? Why is this equilibrium, once attained, lost again, as though forever? What is the source of the feeling we have that we must look after everyone around that moment of calm, that cold moment whose memory is nevertheless strange to us? Why do we know that thing of which there is no knowledge? Imperceptibly the question raises us up, throws us upon one another, is our balance, the balance of a happy day.

The happiness of always saying Yes, of endlessly affirming. We have known other days. Back there, in the past, it seems we walked more quickly, close together we glided more furtively. Toward what place? Why such haste? Sometimes, we look at one another as though between us there were a memory, not a memory—forgetfulness, the touch of an instant, the hope that draws a circle and isolates us. Is it the past—this suddenly visible face?

We knew those days, they don't belong to yesterday, they are eternally those that are coming, those that do not pass, and they are the joy of the brightness that comes from us, and they are the surprise of having breached the wall, and, without error or doubt, going by every road joyously toward ourselves. Why should all that have changed? Why should what had been said, the eternal, cease to be said?

"But nothing has changed. It's only that you also have to know

eternity in the past. You have to raise yourself high enough to be able to say: that was. Such is the mission now reserved for you."

I don't believe in that speech, but I don't have the power to avoid it either. It is as though I had to hear it in the past too, and I feel that not to believe it is to fall more quickly than it is falling down the slope it has already dug.

Spirit of lightness, it must not be betrayed. It is when one moves away from it that the feeling of a constant thought turns into the feeling of an unmoving surveillance. It still protects, but it also bears down—"lightly": it couldn't bear down more than the gravity toward which we let ourselves fall. And where would we fall, if we fell a little more? If we were capable of becoming terribly, guiltily heavy? Isn't that question already the weight that could precipitate us, make us tumble, into an answer?

The answer is that perhaps we would fall back into the calm from which one doesn't emerge except through lightness, because in it everything becomes infinitely light, too light to remain there.

"But aren't they afraid to say, to hear it said, that they're dead?"

"No, why would we be afraid? On the contrary, it's reassuring."

"That proves their insouciance, their boundless frivolity."

"But that's just what death is, being light."

I ask myself why such dialogues seem to hide a deep concern. Motionless thought, thought that wraps me around and perhaps protects me, intractable thought that doesn't answer, that is simply there, you who do not get up, grave, solitary thought in which that point is no doubt hidden, the extremely fine, amazingly distant point that keeps inviting me, without violence, but with a cold authority, to withdraw into forgetfulness. I want to talk to you, you who do not answer. I am allowed to. I will talk calmly, slowly, without interrupting myself, even if I don't talk, even if I have no relation to the speech I am capable of uttering. Why isn't everything over? Why can I question you? Why are you there like a space in which I am still lingering and with which I feel connected? You are not even silent; indifferent to everything, even to silence, and when I go toward you, with a movement that surprises me: a cold, intimate, strange contact—as though I weren't supposed to, as though I couldn't, think of myself.

Why do you let me believe that if I wanted you to, you could become visible? Why do you let me talk to you using intimate words that separate me from everyone else? Are you protecting me? Are you watching me? Why not discourage me? That would be easy, a sign, a firmer pressure, and I would be ready to say: "All right, since you want me to, I'm giving it up." But you are simply there, and the words that go to you go to a wall that sends them back to me so that I can hear them. A wall, a real wall, four walls that form the boundaries of the place I live and make it a cell, an emptiness in the midst of everyone else. Why? What is this role I have to play? What is expected of me? Haven't I, didn't I enter the calm? What has drawn me out of the calm? Could the calm be destroyed? And yet, if it is destroyed, do we continue to keep watch around it—that instant, that cold moment which we don't remember? And is it true that everyone is watching? Maybe only one, maybe no one, maybe we aren't watching over anything, maybe we're all still inside the calm, in that place where we come and go, come and go, ever tottering, ever more restless, and yet this is the breathing of profound repose.

"Calm, calm, what do you want from me?"

"Yes, ask questions, the calm likes that." Why that word? Strange image: it says when a person enters this intimate calm at the moment of dying, at a time when peace and silence have found their place, that person, far from enjoying the calm for himself alone, hands it over to the common spirit by a mysterious gift, doesn't give it up, but hands it over freely—it couldn't be won, taken, or taken by surprise. And the last judgment is perhaps this pure gift through which, in the end, each person always rids himself of his moment of repose. But this calm which penetrates us, which yields us the truth that impels us, the moving force that unites us, this source that is fed by each person when he dies, is, however, the thing we dare not call the eternal heart. Strange, strange thought; I look it in the face, but nothing disturbs it, therefore nothing forbids it, nothing requires it either. Within you, who envelop us and perhaps protect us, who are motionless, solitary and grave, how light thoughts are, how they immediately rise, and all of them are that way—they are all innocent, happy, joyful, the smile and salvation of a moment of emptiness. Nothing sweeter than such thoughts, they are free, they leave us free, to think them is to think nothing, and in this way we question on and on without end.

Why do I have confidence only in you? I feel connected only to you, and even though behind you is hidden the point which is the sky, the empty, ever emptier torment which, through its barely perceptible, eternal pressure, tirelessly urges me to retreat, a calm that no longer draws me but pushes me back, I feel, when I address you, when I question you, when I am able to say, "I question you, I address you," a firmness that safeguards me from the drunkenness that always says *We*. If you are deceiving me, I want you to. If you are nothing, I will be nothing only with you. If what you expect from me is to exhaust you, to give you back to the emptiness that I am, with your help, if that is the ultimate goal, I will reach it.

Note that I am not excluding the idea of the trap you

might represent. Perhaps I'm not dead, and you're here to obtain from me, by your patience and reserve, which I believe in, the free sacrifice of the moment of calm that is to come. The calm is given, it can't be taken back, it is not given, it is the fruit of the last labor, the blooming and balancing that death receives for an instant from itself in the person who is dying. This is the way it is. You won't deny it, nor will you deny that if that instant were left to the person who reached it, there wouldn't be any other instants for him. But the calm must pour into the heart, therefore the mysterious gift, the free judgment, must be accomplished: oh, the happiness of always saying Yes, the surprise of these new bonds and the certainty of what is older; the appeal for a new lightness that comes to me from the first lightness, the thought that is not thought by me, that is already returning to the upper reaches, leading me up with a mad promptness, not altogether leading me up.

Experience, in this case, proves that you protect me by your gravity, which holds me back, that you protect me or cut me off from that shared exaltation, from that shared insouciance, from the immense speech which, as soon as it reaches me, turns into a feeling of infinite joy, and if it falls silent, it does not fall silent, it traverses me, I abide near it, and I also hear myself in that chorus whose base I would like to situate over there, somewhere near the sea. Yet why do you, who give me nothing, promise me nothing, and perhaps conceal the wiliness and the tip of a torment—why do you seem to me to be above what is highest, to be happier than all happiness, more just than balance itself—and what are you? A little space, a point in space?

As you know, there is someone inside this cell. I would rather not talk about it. I believe it is an image. Against you, motionless thought, everything that is reflected in us of everyone comes to assume form, shine, and then disappear. In this way we have the most people, in this way everyone is reflected in each of us by an infinite glimmering that projects us into a radiant intimacy from which each returns to himself, illuminated by being no more than a reflection of everyone else. And the thought that each of us is only the reflection of the universal reflection, this answer to our lightness, makes us drunk with that lightness, makes us ever lighter, lighter than ourselves, in the infinitely glimmering sphere which, from its surface to its single spark, is our own eternal coming and going.

Why do we think that? Because we think everything, every thought is ours, and even the heaviest, once it touches us, quickly becomes light enough to rise and take us with it.

Propped against you, thought against which I rest, my forehead on which my forehead lies heavy, impassable gravity that yields sometimes, nevertheless, to give me a feeling of the past, very cold space in which sterile space returns to space. Why must I keep you, you who keep me? It is a great concern. To live this way in everything so far from everything, and to sustain lightness as a weight, to address words to you that don't reach you, don't express me—and to hold you fast so that you remain strictly delimited, a little chamber where someone has to live.

I have to hold you fast, watch your boundaries. I have to overcome the suspicion that there is no repose in your immobility and your enduring presence is an endless withdrawal. Is it me you're moving away from—these thoughts I don't have, these words that don't reach you? Are you trying to warn me of some danger? Would you like to speak? You're becoming upset, you're becoming upset, I feel it. It makes me upset too.

I lay down for a moment. What calm next to you. What

emptiness here. It seemed to me we were silent. A memory of light comes in through the little window, and it's a cold brightness that penetrates everywhere, that creates the emptiness and is the brightness of that emptiness. I remember that room well, a room whose boundaries you define strictly, with your characteristic rigor, and which I can't leave, because it is already dominated by the outside. How exact everything is, more exact than it should be. You are acquainted with shadows. How strange that the darkness of the night should be this motionless, solitary brightness. I could describe to you the space that you form, perhaps without knowing it, and if I lean outside, I see the hallway lit by the light; if I go out into it, already my steps come to meet me. But I won't go out. All these people I see wandering about, these similar figures obeying the murmur of the night, which says one must come and go, come and go without end: deceptive faith, pointless haste, delusion that is the night's very breathing. Why such haste? Toward what place? Do my words also go toward that place, taking some unknown part of me with them? I sense, in them, that attraction to the vain region, but why do you prevent me from flowing into this murmur? Why do you save me from being entirely outside myself, why do you separate me from what speaks in me, as though to deflect me, for an instant, from the delusion into which everything goes, from which everything comes back? What part do I have in the words that entreat me with a sweet lure to follow them and that I resist only because you enclose me—but I'm afraid I won't always resist them. One day, I will say a word I don't know but which will perhaps be the sign that I am renouncing the calm that awaits me—and might you be there to lead me to say that word? Have you assumed the face and the form of what I love in order to obtain it freely from me? Who are you? You can't be what you are. But you are someone. Then, who?

I ask this. I don't even ask it. But our words are so light that they keep opening out into questions.

It wouldn't take much for me to begin believing in my separate existence again and for me to add faith to the truth of images. However, I know that that would be to remember, and the time in which one can say *I* is limited, perilous. It is like a flame coming to light on one or the other of us and designating him to answer the general speech. Then what is happening? What issues from the earth is a strange voice, a stifled murmur, a dry, arid cry; this disturbs us, obliges us to hear, and who utters it? What is that single word on which the heaviness still in us concentrates and falls back, a too weighty feeling that breaks the circle and frees itself? Is it true that we can't love each other, that we are too light for that, too joined together in our lightness?

Perhaps I have entered into forbidden relations with you that I can't explain. Somehow, where you are is the suffering I haven't been able to suffer, a suffering that drives the darkness and memory of life back to the edges. This must be what makes you so grave and solitary despite the bonds that unite us—but that weigh on you, I am afraid, and what connects us? Indifference, perhaps; necessity, perhaps; it has no name. For a long time I have sensed that you suffer, with a suffering that I don't sense, but that is in your silent brightness, that is no doubt that brightness itself, an even, shadowless light that penetrates everything and keeps me outside everything. I would like to preserve you from it. I, too, feel, though from a distance, a great distance, and as though it were a complicity that passes painfully outside of me, the link between the suffering and what ought to be my thought.

There is a rumor which says that at a certain moment, the slow fire consuming the other world will make manifest its internal movement and secret unity. The fire burns only in order to bring to light the living plan of the great edifice, destroys it but in keeping with its unity, reveals it as it consumes it. The belief that the great edifice is now no longer capable of feeding a central fire strong enough to illuminate everything in a general blaze. The belief that one has reached the moment when everything is burning, when everything is randomly extinguished in myriad different hearths working where they like, as they like, with the cold passion of separate fires. The belief that we might be the gleaming signs of the fire's writing, written in everyone, legible only in me, the one who answers the general certainty—but that was at an earlier time and that was each of us—with his murmur. The belief that this belief is nothing more than the sadness and suffering of the fire, which has become too weak and already nearly broken.

Perhaps we don't love, perhaps we can't very easily tolerate the thought of the mysterious order whose fortuitous wonder, whose surprise, the surprise of eternal chance, we affirm through the caprice that is in us.

Could you really be the presence—motionless, collected, and extended through space—of the possibly infinite pain that exists in a single thought? Is it in you that I might still suffer—in you, and so very far from myself—ever since suffering moved beyond me, as though, in a gift I can't explain to myself, I had given you the suffering I couldn't accept and even the sadness that can no longer sadden me? Might the arrow I didn't hold back try to find you, a target that would grant it rest? This doesn't allow itself to be held back either, and I have to confess that I don't think I'm still capable of suffering, or even of encountering the briefest instant of pain. I don't know why that word appeared here, I don't know what it describes or what force keeps it here. I'm sorry that sadness, pain have been given to thought, but no doubt it's the law. The little thoughts are all the lighter because of it, and we are closer to ourselves, closer to everything, more exalted in the calm that is our belief and our subsistence. Even when I say I would like to preserve you from it, how coldly, how lightly I say it, without taking part in it. How cold I am already, and yet it isn't said completely in vain.

Thought which allows me to be without suffering, thought in which I suffer so very far away from myself, to the point where I don't exist, you who have a torment in the center of your transparency that you hide from us: don't think I'm indifferent to your fate, I pay more attention to it than I should. But consider how vain, light, insignificant, truthless we are already, and always unsteady, always saying what never stops being said. Day and night, day and night. We're over there, and the absence of secrecy is our condition. Even where impenetrability reigns, all the more impenetrable as it draws back moment by moment under pressure from you, nothing is secret, nothing is revealed that wasn't revealed in the beginning. And yet, with you, I would like to talk in secret, in secret in relation to everyone, in secret in relation to you. It is like a new desire. It is in me like a future taking me by surprise.

Don't hold it against me, and don't think I want to exert a power of indiscretion and influence over you. It is understood that between us, every answer is excluded. I wouldn't like you to be able to answer me, and I'm happy with your silence, which doesn't answer, which doesn't even draw me into silence. Answering belongs to a region that the two of us must have left a very long time ago. How could I question you, if every answer hadn't already dissipated?

It's true that I would like to come near, but without wanting to, and does that mean near you? To look for you in you? To keep watch in your place? Though I'm not sure of it, I clearly see that the space between us is growing. It is still only emptiness, but the little room is larger, more difficult to embrace in a single memory. It seems to me you're struggling against something over there, so far away from everything, and your struggle is solitary, motionless, discreet, and unrelated to our spirit of lightness, which you preserve with your incomprehensible gravity. Why are you struggling, and why over there? Why that shivering which, though it may be pain in you, is drunkenness in us? Surely, the little thoughts that are so light for us are less so for you, and you suffer from their delicious dispersal, which yields neither forgetfulness nor memory. What can I do for you? How can I make the moment easier for you? What is being prolonged in you that no longer has any importance for me? Would you like to offer death—which is only real, they say, for all of us together, in that speech of exaltation that we contain together—the one thought that would give it a sweet equality with you, with itself? Believe me, that is superfluous. Even if a shared death results in doubts about the death of each of us, about mine in particular, too bad. Uncertain, I very easily put up with that uncertainty, which is too fragile to disturb me—and wouldn't it be a pity to try to appropriate such an old event for myself, one that so scarcely belongs to me? Together, it has no attraction or truth except in the place where we hold it together, raised up toward us by the force of insouciance that scatters us among ourselves and reunites us in it. What would you want to balance against that thought of a shared death? As you see, you have trouble containing it, and I imagine I would only have to affirm it a little more to make you yield, but also that it is thrust almost disdainfully out of those confines where you remain and where it barely arrives.

You don't like it that I accept the uncertainty I am filled with so lightly—I even accept it joyfully. But what do you

want? One can't have large and small certainties. I am surrounded by questions. They all point, some with a barbaric
rigidity, others with nonchalance, toward the center I took
over, jealously enclosing myself within the circle where I am
the only one who knows there is no one there. I know everything, I know everything. Don't you admire this uncertainty,
which owes nothing to ignorance? And the calm, too, is
uncertain, in whose midst we are reborn ceaselessly into our
own lightness: a large question, steady, indestructible, perhaps entrusted to our negligence. It mustn't be betrayed.

There are spots here that your light illuminates, others it
also illuminates, others it also illuminates with an even light. I
might be able to see lots of interesting details out the window,
but I'm not curious about those things: it's enough for me to
know we're over there, and my curiosity would be more likely
to turn me away from there. It is a great deal to be illuminated
on all sides this way, at every instant, by a light that comes
from nowhere, that only attracts images, then pushes them
away, attracts light thoughts, then pushes them away. I'm
not sure that brightness has any relation to you. I'm inclined
to believe that you don't illuminate, that you keep yourself
within confines where the darkness whitens, without another
day appearing. I recognize that I'm lying down in that pit of
light, whose boundaries are so strictly defined except at one
point. Remember: the eyes are shut, and the mouth is also
shut. It probably happened in the room. Under my eyelids I
had the deep black, velvety, rich, and warm, that sleep preserves, that dreams always feel reappearing behind them;
and no doubt I was already dead in many parts of myself, but
the black was still alive. It went on for a long time, maybe
forever. I remained close to the black, maybe in it. I waited
without impatience, lightly I watched for the moment when
the black would lose its color and inevitably, by losing it,

cause the final whiteness to rise. The last day, the sun of the dead. Maybe this is the very same white light in which I am immersed.

I would very much like you to merge with it or at least foretell it, you who lie in wait, beyond what arrives, for what doesn't arrive. Are you the black that dies away little by little and allows the illusion to see clearly for an instant? Or are you only the patience that prepares me for it, also prepares me to renounce it? Is this black point which we call the sky, which keeps drawing back, growing thinner—is it all that is left to me of the living black in which I passed away? It's not much. And you—are you fighting to keep it going or to dissipate it? To announce the evidence that follows it or to denounce it? Strange, strange pain—that very separate thought.

In that case, would this cold transparency be the night? Like a day of snow. Would it be the black following the black without corruption or strange vision?

Know that I don't want things to be prolonged. I'm not tired of them—on the contrary, I am without fatigue, without the obstinacy there is in fatigue. Attached to you, who are only detachment. Light with the weight you will load onto me. I know very well that you don't exist anyway, and that this is what reunites us. But it is in this that I also risk uniting with you, without dream and without image, through a movement whose old ruses I remember. Edge of the empty brightness, over which you keep watch: it musn't be altered.

Sometimes I feel I am the great thought, and you are the assault on it led by the desire not to think, even though you perpetually oppose me.

Why don't you want to think me? Is it powerlessness, indifference, blind will? Are you on one side and I on the other? Are both of us the same thought, similarly grave, solitary and motionless, which this separate identity pushes back forever one from the other, strangers so as not to be confused and so as to maintain the equality of the balance? Are you in the night the thought that I am in the other night? Are you the only one speaking, asking me all the questions I answer only with a silence that doesn't answer? Are you always the serious thought of earlier times that I have outdistanced? Could you still be over there?

Bitter, bitter thought, then I would be where you are not yet, I would be the large *me* against which you are struggling by not letting yourself think it, the great certainty within which you find no room, which therefore doesn't understand you in particular. Maybe the question of knowing if I am already, and you not yet, can't be broached. I think it wouldn't change anything between us. This doubt—bitter, bitter, I recognize that—is only a form of the lightness that keeps charming us. And if I am apparently lighter than you, I am so, not because I unloaded myself of all burdens, but because I am light with that weight you constantly load onto me, the weight of refusal and forgetting which you are.

So long as there exists a relationship of intimacy between us that allows me to address you, I have the feeling you will remain yourself. But despite everything, you shouldn't trust my advances too much. I form a doubt about myself greater than what you can tolerate. And who is talking? Is it you? Is it me in you? Is it the murmur that keeps passing between us and whose different echoes reach us from shore to shore? Oh, how you shiver, how you seem to flee before the agitation which I draw you toward, in this case, by turning it away.

We shouldn't be afraid. What separates us is infinitesimal, anyway: a moment of calm, a moment of horror, but calm.

Notice that I'm not giving in to the ease of regarding you as the last thought, the thought which opened space when I left it, and perhaps keeps it open in order to let me go eternally by holding me back. Let that not be. If you were my last thought, our relations would quickly cease to be tolerable. It would be very distressing to imagine that what is fixed about your presence, and the sharp point you hide, the emptiness around which you gather yourself with an inflexible authority, all that, which makes you as motionless and sure as the sky, came from a thought which can no longer change, a thought on which you remained pierced, pinned as though on yourself, by that closure of suffering which refuses to speak.

Might you suffer, then, from being a very little thought, instead of the vast thought into which you wanted to issue forth? Very little thought, I like you this way. Whatever the thought, the end makes it vibrate to infinity, to immensity, by a slip that your strictness must of course reject as illusory. Or does this immensity itself seem still not enough for you, mediocre and shabby by comparison to the point you preserve, the point on which you close yourself again in a terrible contraction?

Why don't you want to give in? Why do you tirelessly reduce this immensity to a simplicity which is like a face, where you are, that I might be able to see? Don't you want to have the night, the night I am for you, as you are for me, the night in which you would sink down and place yourself exactly on top of yourself, answer to your question, question whose answer you will be? We must melt into each other. What is an end for you will surely be a beginning in me. Aren't you tempted by the happiness of the circle? You go before me, a loving memory, a recollection of what hasn't taken place. You go before me like a hope, yet I am also what you must rejoin, and it is in me that you will be able to rejoin yourself. Think about that, add it to the extreme thought.

It is true that I, too, still have the desire to talk to you as to a face confronting me over there on the horizon. Invisible face. The space of that face always more invisible, and, between us, the calm. It is as though I had died in order to recall this, in order to take desire and memory as far as possible. Could it be that one dies in order to recall something? Could you be the intimacy of that memory? Do I have to talk so that you will place yourself just opposite me? And you—don't you feel the need to be, one last time, near the calm, that thin, closed face? Last possibility of being looked at by the great thought, the great certainty.

I think this is what tempts us both: I, that you be a face, what is visible in a face, and you, to be a face for me once more, to be a thought and yet a face. The desire to be visible in the night, so that it will invisibly fade away.

But the lament I suddenly hear—in me? In you? *"Eternal, eternal; if we are eternal, how could we have been? How can we be tomorrow?"*

He said there is always a moment when remembering and dying—being dead, perhaps—coincide. The movement would be the same. A pure, directionless memory, in which everything becomes memory. A great power of which one would only have to know how to avail oneself in order to die of memory. But an unavailable power. Therefore, the unfortunate attempt to recall oneself to oneself, the retreat, the retreat before forgetfulness and the retreat before death, which remembers.

What does it remember? Itself, death as memory. An immense memory in which one dies.

First to forget. To remember only where one remembers nothing. To forget: to remember everything as though by way of forgetting. There is a profoundly forgotten point from which every memory radiates. Everything is exalted in memory from something which is forgotten, an infinitesimal detail, a minuscule fissure into which it passes in its entirety.

If I must eventually forget, if I must remember you only by forgetting you, if it is said that he who will remember will be profoundly forgotten by himself and by that memory which he will not distinguish from his forgetting, if, already, for a long time now, I sense that I will only reach you mingled with him and confused with the images that hide him from himself, then know this . . .

Memory that I am, yet that I also wait for, toward which I go down toward you, far from you, space of that memory, of which there is no memory, which holds me back only where I have long since ceased to be, as though you, who perhaps do not exist, in the calm persistence of what disappears, were continuing to turn me into a memory and search for what could recall me to you, great memory in which we are both held fast, face to face, wrapped in the lament I hear: *Eternal, eternal*; space of cold light into which you have drawn me without being there and in which I affirm you without seeing you, knowing that you are not there, not knowing it, knowing it. Growth of what cannot grow, vain waiting for vain things, silence, and the more silence there is, the more it changes into a clamor. Silence, silence that makes so much noise, perpetual agitation of the calm—is this what we call the terrible thing, the eternal heart? Is this what we keep watch over in order to soothe it, to make it calm, ever calmer, to prevent it from stopping, from persevering? Could it be that for myself, I am that terrible thing? To be dead and still be waiting for something that turns you into a memory of death.

Waiting, waiting for a face. Strange that space can still hold such waiting. Strange that what is darkest should have this great desire to look at a face. Here, there are many of them, it's true. Some are very beautiful, all have at least a certain beauty and a few, as far as I have been able to notice in the hallway, are wonderfully attractive, perhaps to the extent that they themselves, in the calm and the silence, are under the sway of the essential attraction. But this isn't quite what I want. Maybe there are many faces, but only one face, neither beautiful, nor friendly, nor hostile, simply visible: the face I imagine you are, even the face you certainly are, because of the refusal to appear that exists in you, because of the grave motionlessness, the rectitude that never turns away, the transparency that cannot let itself be disturbed. And only what is disturbed can appear.

Sometimes it seems that certain faces, by coming together, try to sketch out such a face. It seems that they all eternally rise toward one another to cause that face to be present. It seems that each would like to be the only one for all the others, wanting all to be the only one for it, and to be, for each, all the others. It seems that the emptiness is never empty enough. The images' eternal yearning, the delusion that lifts us up and involves us incessantly in the disorder of the night, lost and always brought together again in an outburst of joy where we find each other again. Illusion, the happiness of the illusion—why resist it? Why can't all these faces mislead me? Why do you keep me away from them by this thought of the space that might make you visible for an instant—more invisible?

Maybe you will be the exception, the brightness that does not grow dark. Maybe you will pass through the doors of terror without the shivering that is calm here, from wave to wave, is the tremor of calm with which we exalt ourselves, light watchkeepers around ourselves. And yet I have to see you. I have to torment you until the great nocturnal space grows quiet for an instant in this face that must confront it. As though it were necessary that you not renounce transparency and that, being bright, you remain ever brighter, a refusal of the unthinkable to the very end, so that there can be seen in you just what the others are losing in their premature happiness at being visible. Too beautiful troubled faces. A face cannot be that. The very last face, merely manifest, beyond waiting and beyond reach. Face which is the emptiness, perhaps. That is why you must watch over empty space in order to preserve it, as I must watch over it to alter it, a fight in which we are together, close through distance, strangers in everything we share, presence where I touch you intact and where you hold me back at a distance, a distance formed of you but which separates me from you: a pit of light, a brightness in which I am buried. Face, face of expectation, yet withdrawn from what is expected, the unexpected of all expectation, the unforeseeable certainty.

Oh, if it is true that we were alive together—and, really, you were already a thought—if it is possible that these words flowing between us tell us something that comes to us from us, at an earlier time wasn't I always, near you, this light, avid, insatiable desire to see you and yet, once you were visible, to transform you further, into something more visible, to draw you, slowly and darkly, into that point where you couldn't any longer be anything but seen, where your face became the nakedness of a face and your mouth metamorphosed into a mouth? Wasn't there a moment when you said to me: "I have the feeling that when you die, I will become completely visible, more visible than is possible and to the point that I won't be able to endure it." Strange, strange speech. Is it now that you say this? Could it be that he is dying at this moment? Is it you who always die in him, near him? Could it be that he wasn't dead enough, calm enough, strange enough, does he have to carry desire, memory even further, is that the extremely fine and amazingly distant point that always slips away and by which, slowly, with authority, you draw him, you push him back into forgetfulness?

Thought, infinitesimal thought, calm thought, pain.

Later, he asked himself how he had entered the calm. He couldn't talk about it with himself. Only joy at feeling he was in harmony with the words: "Later, he . . . "

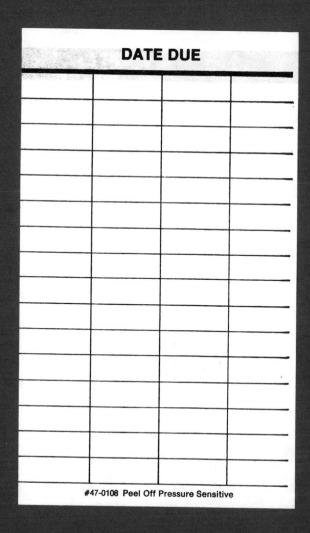